CARIBBEAN WOMEN'S MIGRATION

WINDRUSH ERA HOUSING EXPERIENCES AND ASPIRATIONS

AuthorHouse™ UK
1663 Liberty Drive
Bloomington, IN 47403 USA
www.authorhouse.co.uk
UK TFN: 0800 0148641 (Toll Free inside the UK)
UK Local: 02036 956322 (+44 20 3695 6322 from outside the UK)

Because of the dynamic nature of the Internet, any web addresses or
links contained in this book may have changed since publication and may
no longer be valid. The views expressed in this work are solely those
of the author and do not necessarily reflect the views of the publisher,
and the publisher hereby disclaims any responsibility for them.

Any people depicted in stock imagery provided by Getty Images are models,
and such images are being used for illustrative purposes only.
Certain stock imagery © Getty Images.

This book is printed on acid-free paper.

ISBN: 978-1-6655-9724-1 (sc)
ISBN: 978-1-6655-9725-8 (e)

Print information available on the last page.

Published by AuthorHouse 11/10/2022

author HOUSE®

Caribbean Women's Migration

Windrush Era Housing Experiences and Aspirations

Figure 1: Windrush Square in Brixton, South London

Source: Wikimedia Commons.

12th December 2006 (Original upload date)

Dorrel L. Green-Briggs

CONTENTS

FIGURES AND TABLES

Figures

Tables

PREFACE

Caribbean Women's Migration: Windrush Era Housing Experiences and Aspirations is a qualitative case-study analysis of eight London-based women. The main purpose of the research was to document the housing histories of each subject over half a century since their arrival and subsequent settlement in the United Kingdom. The discourse's main themes look at the following areas:

- The exploration of Caribbean women's migration literature during the *Windrush* period (1948–1970).

- Racial discrimination and Caribbean housing access.

- Analysis of UK and US literature and continued patterns of black and ethnic minority concentration and segregation in inner-city metropolitan areas.

Caribbean *Windrush* women and men have strived to elevate their living standards and have shown resourcefulness in overcoming barriers and achieving their aspirations in acquiring property. Caribbeans are represented within the full spectrum of housing tenure, although presently more are represented in social housing.

Black and ethnic minority segregation and concentration still exist in inner-city regions, that poses an ongoing challenge for well-meaning housing providers.

In looking at de-concentration in favour of mixed communities within cities, for black minority ethnic groups (BME), where there is a preference, this should be supported.

Caribbean women's literature depicting the female *Windrush* experience was practically absent at the time *Windrush* migration was occurring. The documenting of the women's housing case studies has proved to be a fascinating and worthwhile inquiry that gives a voice to Caribbean women who were doubly marginalised as women and because they were black. The case-study research will serve to enlighten and inspire subsequent generations of black, white, and people of all minority ethnicities living in the United Kingdom.

ACKNOWLEDGEMENTS

I would like to dedicate this book to my father, Bertram Ranfurly Green, who although departed, has always been proud of me. I love you always.

A heartfelt tribute is extended to my mother, Bernice Millicent Green, who was extremely supportive in every way imaginable. I have been blessed to have had such a wonderful mother who was my first inspirational interviewee, and has been a guiding star throughout my life and even now. Sadly, she passed away in June 2016, seven years after my father. Fortunately, she was able to see much of this work completed. Without her, the documentary would never have come to fruition.

My abounding appreciation is extended to the Caribbean migration women (Interviewees), for their captivating documentaries and experiences that made this book possible.

To my committed husband, Franklin Basoene Briggs, who is without a doubt my soulmate, thank you for your tireless assistance in getting me where I needed to be and being side by side with me during this process and your positive belief in my capabilities throughout. To my thoughtful children, Reema, Keiran, and Damani. My grandchildren, who are my joy - Kaireece, Kashiem, Ra'shi, Khemeis, and Kasey. To my approving brothers, Barry and Rodney Green.

Thank you to everyone who gave me guidance to be better and to push myself. Namely, Jane Lewis and Patrick Mulrenan, Professors based at London Metropolitan University. Also, my dear friend Sophia Sterling, who made time to read the manuscript and give constructive feedback.

Not forgetting Fr. Charles Card-Reynolds at St Bartholomew's Anglican Church, who gave me sound advice, encouragement, and the support needed to stay the course with my endeavours.

The acknowledgements would not be complete without a very special expression of my unequivocal appreciation to Sandra A. Agard, for her deeply moving, eloquent and complimentary Foreword. I can honestly say that Ms. Agard was the one and only choice from the very beginning.

The first time I read her poem – *A House* it resonated with me, tying in with the Caribbean Migration women's documentaries and translated honestly the housing experiences of Caribbean women, children and men in multi-occupancy private lodging houses at that time, through a little girl's eyes. Agard's poem ignited a passion within, and from that moment I felt deeply connected to her even though we weren't formally acquainted. When I became committed to publishing my dissertation into a book, it was necessary for me to trace Agard. I did go to quite some lengths to connect with her, it was a must. I'll admit for a wee moment I nearly lost hope; but at last, I received an email response, the connection was made, and it was electric! Our conversations flowed effortlessly, she has a warm, engaging and positively charming disposition, but most importantly she understood my mission and was totally on board.

Agard is an inspiration to me. Her literary accomplishments span over three decades as an author, storyteller, book doctor and literature and oral consultant. She is passionate about preserving black African-Caribbean legacy and giving a voice to the voiceless and especially black female voices that were often stifled. This is a passion of which we share a common ground.

Thank you, Sandra Agard, for your belief in me and my work and for giving me a platform. I am eternally grateful and honoured.

FOREWORD

Dorrel Green-Briggs's study on Caribbean Women's Migration: Windrush Era Housing Experiences and Aspirations opens with acknowledgements to her parents – Betram Ranfurly Green and Bernice Millicent Green. The acknowledgements continue to thank her husband, Franklin Basoene Briggs. Then there are the children, the grandchildren, her siblings, all those who gave her guidance 'to stay the course'. What a course indeed a journey Green-Briggs has been on, for in this qualitative case-study analysis of eight London-based women and the history behind Caribbean migration to the United Kingdom from the 1940s. She gives voices to the voiceless as she tells their untold stories.

Stories of Caribbean Women's Migration and their traumatic experiences in housing and their aspirations of which there were many. Aspirations that for many were not realised due to the blatant racism and/or official legislation by the host country. A host country who had openly invited Caribbean people to the UK in order to help rebuild post war Britain. Many would leave families behind – parents, husbands, wives, and children. Thereby fracturing families – relationships. Many would never see their own parents ever again. That indeed is yet another story amongst many.

At the heart of these stories is Family and therefore it is more than fitting that Green-Briggs's work opens up with acknowledgments of family and friends. Theirs are the shoulders she has stood on – without them she would not have been able to go on this journey as she searched for answers to the fundamental question – what were the experiences of those early pioneers of the Windrush Generation as:

Caribbean Windrush women and men have strived to elevate their living standards and have shown resourcefulness in overcoming barriers and achieving their aspirations in acquiring property.

The starting point, the inspiration as she calls it for Green-Briggs were her parents – 'recollections of my parents' memories of migration from Jamaica during the 1950s'.

This is for her and indeed all of us, who have borne witness to the consequences of the migration of parents and grandparents from the Caribbean in the 1950s, is the heart of the story.

Green-Briggs acknowledges the 'importance of sustaining cultural heritage and identity', which for her, for all of us with Caribbean ancestry – 'brought a sense of pride'.

As a Literature Consultant, I often employ literature to highlight my own work. Green-Briggs does this too and in doing so illustrates that much of the migration literature is written from a male viewpoint. She rightly identifies the importance of works like Peter Fryer's, Staying Power: The History of Black People in Britain and Samuel Selvon's The Lonely Londoners in illustrating the experiences of the Caribbean community as they negotiated this 'strange land' called England.

What Green-Briggs I feel accomplishes so successfully is identifying a host of other sources that examines the history of housing for the Caribbean migration and for women especially.

The Caribbean ex-servicemen were initially identified as the first migrant passenger group on board HMS Windrush. The women migrants were overlooked according to the writing of James and Harris. They identified up to 600 West Indian women recruited for the Auxiliary Territorial Service (ATS) – many of who arrived in November 1943. Their important stories are untold.

As I say repeatedly, Green-Briggs gives a voice to untold stories by delving deeply to find the histories that have been well documented; but side-lined in the writing of this period.

Histories like Stephen Bourne's War to Windrush: Black Women in Britain 1939 to 1948, which examines:

'...the West Indian women's sense of duty and commitment to king and mother country. This commitment would inspire them to pay their own fares to come to England to be of service'.

Caribbean women like Constance Goodridge Mark aka Connie Mark, whose contribution to the war effort has finally begun to see the light of day.

Connie documented her own story and that of her compatriots by keeping diaries and taking photos. She recalls the surprise of her audience at an Age Concern meeting when she would produce this evidence of hers and others' contributions to the war effort. Her audience had no idea that there were Black servicewomen in the war; in fact, I had no idea either.

I was a student who studied British History to A level standard but was never taught this vital information about the Second World War. I like so many others students would discover these stories from other sources – reading beyond the set texts. I would also attend and participate as a young writer in cultural events like The International Book Fair of Radical Black and Third World Books in the eighties and nineties.

I was fortunate to attend several events featuring the delightful and charismatic Connie Mark. Her stories of the war effort were electric, courageous and inspiring. I will never forget them and the pride that she instilled in us, her eager audiences as she told us her truths about the war and her and others' outstanding contributions to it. Her truths filled in the gaps where Black women's stories are so often missing.

However, much to her credit, Green-Briggs does not only stop at Connie Mark, she gives us a host of Caribbean women who had contributed to the war effort. All this before the arrival of HMT (His Majesty Transport) Empire Windrush on 22 June 1948. Or, indeed HMS Ormonde that arrived the year before in 1947 with 110 Jamaican workers – a fact that is commonly overlooked.

Green-Briggs examines the consequences of the well-documented recruitment programmes of the British Government that brought the Caribbean people to work on public transport and in hospitals.

These men and women were recruited in the Caribbean to help rebuild post war Britain by the British Government and British companies like London Transport and, the newly formed National Health Service. It is important that such information is made readily available in schools and in history books as they paint a different truth of Britain in the 1940s to 1960s.

Caribbean Windrush women and men have strived to elevate their living standards and have shown resourcefulness in overcoming barriers and achieving their aspirations in acquiring property despite the many obstacles that were constantly put in their way like the banks not giving them mortgages.

There are so many factors to admire about Green-Briggs's work for not only does she examine closely Caribbean migration but the reasons for it in the first place. Yes, there was the active official recruitment drives of British companies like London Transport, but what was actually in the Caribbean itself?

The picture that is presented of the Caribbean is one of instability and hardship as sugar production – one of the main sources of income for the Caribbean islands – was falling rapidly due to the slow rebuilding process after the war and the underdevelopment of the islands.

The irony is that there was a demand for the product but a lack of shipping caused the industry to fall into decline. Coupled with the need for modernisation of the sugar industry and the drain of the work force as many migrated to the UK – the islands were left depleted and the consequences of this drain of resources of people and industries are still being felt to this day in the Caribbean – but that's another story to be told another day.

As always, Green-Briggs gives an historical context to a contemporary story. By citing the British Nationality Act of 1948, whereby British colonial subjects were eligible to claim British Citizenship which allowed Caribbean peoples' rightful entry to Britain without a visa. They were in effect British citizens and so arrived optimistic and eager to work and improve their economic and educational status like my parents, Green-Briggs herself and so many others. Many people were left sadly disillusioned and disappointed by the hostile reception they received from the host country.

Housing was an ongoing issue. Discrimination would play a key role as the Caribbean migrates sought adequate accommodation.

Here Green-Briggs uses Caribbean literature, poetry and creative writing to illustrate post war Britain.

She uses the rediscovered writings of the pioneer and trailblazer, Beryl Gilroy, one of the first Black head teachers in the UK. In doing so we see how discrimination had influenced her early life in London as she struggles to get work as a teacher and as publisher writer.

Green-Briggs also uses my own autobiographical poem, *A House* to highlight the living conditions in inner city London. This prose poem's story is told through the eyes of a child, and highlights the life of a family living in two rooms – just about surviving in effect. However, to a young child the struggles of her family are not apparent as she recalls her playing with her two sisters, school days, the treats, TV programmes, the parties, letters from Home/Guyana, the food, Christmas. It is a golden fun-filled time for a child, not so much for a parent.

It was both an honour and a delight to see my poem written over thirty years ago included in this study and I would like to thank Dorrel Green-Briggs for doing so. As she says, 'it strikes a familiar chord' then and now.

In this section there are additional Caribbean women's voices namely – the Jamaican Storyteller and Poet, Louise Bennett and the Trinidadian Political Activist and Journalist Founder of the Notting Hill Carnival and West Indian Gazette newspaper, Claudia Jones. This demonstrates fully that during this period there were women's voices both documenting and bearing witness to the ongoing situations – if only they were fully acknowledged at the time. It shows these women's resilience. For regardless of the ongoing discrimination, they would record their stories.

And, these women would eventually buy their own houses. As the women and their families were not awarded mortgages by the banks - they would ask the community through schemes like 'pardner' – a saving system partnership to save collectively.

By bringing all these stories here, we can see the depth of, and sheer value of these histories that have been invisible for far too long.

On a very personal note, I would like to add that when I studied for my Masters in the mid-nineties I had an unpleasant time, which clearly reflects the lack of Black Women's Voices in British History and the constant battles for inclusion with the establishment.

My dissertation was on Black Women's Oral History. My supervisor tried her best to deter me from doing this subject. I literally had to fight tooth and nail to get it through. There always seems to be a struggle...a story – one to be told another day.

In conclusion, Dorrel Green-Briggs gives a comprehensive depiction of post war Britain and the impact of Caribbean migration and especially Black women. She uses numerous first-hand accounts with the qualitative case-study analysis of eight London-based women and the history behind Caribbean migration to the United Kingdom from the 1940s. Green-Briggs illustrates comprehensively the mood of post war Britain as it endeavoured to rebuild itself.

More importantly, Green-Briggs has given a voice indeed voices to countless Black Women by highlighting housing as she links missing histories, weaving stories together to fill in the gaps in Caribbean and British Histories.

This work will easily fit into the canons of Social, Cultural and Political of British Histories. It will now have the Voices of Caribbean Women firmly embedded within it.

Dorrel Green-Briggs began by thanking family and friends in her acknowledgments. I would like to thank her for giving the world this exciting, ground breaking and inspiring body of work. It is a much-needed addition to Caribbean, British and World Histories.

Give Thanks and Praise Always.

Asè O.

Sandra A. Agard Hon FRSL

August 2022

Author, Storyteller, Book Doctor, Literature and Oral Consultant.

CHAPTER 1
_____

Introduction

1.1 Background

The inspiration that led to the research of _Windrush_ women's housing experiences commenced with recollections of my parents' memories of migration from Jamaica during the 1950s. Acknowledging the importance of sustaining memories of cultural heritage and identity brought a sense of pride.

The notion of preserving Caribbean identity is not a new phenomenon. Therefore, a gap within the research needed to be identified. After some inspection, it became noticeable that the literature available about Windrush migration mainly speaks of Caribbean men's experiences (Fryer 1984). Migration literature was written from a male viewpoint, such as depicted in Sam Selvon's novel _The Lonely Londoners_ (1956).

Compiling the women's case studies, with an extensive coverage of their housing history, was a committed and challenging process. Eight women's case studies were successfully completed. This is an essential area of inquiry as it gives a voice to women who were under-documented.

Caribbean ex-servicemen were the majority migrant passenger group aboard the _Windrush_ and journeying to the United Kingdom, especially in the earlier years. Therefore, it was the men's (Imperial War Museum 2014) presence that was being reported (Fryer 1984). The presence of women migrants was minor, and their voices were often muted (James and Harris 1993).

Caribbean Women in WWII

It has been estimated that there may have been up to 600 potential West Indian women recruits signed up for the (ATS) Auxiliary Territorial Service. (The Black Presence in Britain 2022) _Refer to Figure 2._ Many arriving in November 1943. The actual number of West Indian female recruits cannot be accurately confirmed as pointed out by Stephen Bourne (2018). These women's sense of duty and commitment to King and mother country would inspire 381 black women from the

Caribbean to pay their own fares to come to England to be of service during World War II. (Bourne, 2018: 89) Undoubtedly a number of these women (if not all), faced challenges as women in addition to colour discrimination and being an immigrant, recruit in the war office establishment. Despite the obstacles, they persevered and proved their capabilities and excelled. Many of their stories have now been preserved as a lasting reminder and legacy in Black British history. Women such as Constance Goodridge Mark or aka (Connie Mark), born in Jamaica and who years later remarked, when relaying her story at an Age Concern meeting, where she produced photographs of herself and other West Indian female service women colleagues, the level of surprise and intrigue that it created, Connie stated:

> that it caused such a stir, people said, we never knew there were black ex-servicewomen and that we even came to England. (The Black Presence in Britain, 2022)

There were other ATS women documented such as Barbadian born Marjorie and Odessa Gittens; Louise Osborne from St. Lucia and Miss L. Curtis born in Bermuda. (Bourne, 2018: 87, 89; The Black Presence in Britain, 2022) Prior to the recruitment of ATS Caribbean service women, there had already been black women in occupation at the ATS. Possibly twenty or so as well as roughly half a dozen black British women stationed at the WAAF: Women's Auxiliary Air Force. This would include black British born Lilian Bader who came from the home region of Liverpool and joined the WAAF in 1941. (Bourne, 2018: 89)

Figure 2: Military Service Women

Caribbean ATS Recruits

Caribbean women, although generally receiving less exposure than Caribbean men, also played their part contributing in the war effort.

Source: Hulton Archive/Getty Images. Photo by Central Press

Figure 3: *Empire Windrush,* London

[1]The S.S. *Empire Windrush*

Source: Hulton Getty Archive. Photo by Daily Herald Archive

---

[1] The *Empire Windrush,* docking at Tilbury, Essex, on 22 June 1948, marks the beginning of many voyages packed with Caribbean migrants seeking to improve their financial condition and be of service to the mother country (Phillips 2011).

Figure 3.1: The *Empire Windrush* Docked at Tilbury

Source: Hulton Getty Archive. Photo by Douglas Miller

The SS *Empire Windrush*, which had formerly been a German cruise boat (Cavendish 2014), docked on 22 June 1948. Comprising of 492 official passengers, not including stowaways (Cavendish 2014; Patterson 1965; Fryer 1984). Courtman (2012) argues that the figure of 492 passengers that has been circulated over the years is inaccurate and a ploy from the beginning to alleviate the British host anxieties about Caribbean migration (Courtman 2012). The *Empire Windrush* was not the first ship to anchor on UK shores carrying Caribbean passengers. Harris (see James and Harris 1993) describes the 1947 arrival of the *Ormonde* with 110 Jamaican workers, including ten stowaways. (Also, see Interviewee 8's account of her husband's arrival to the England in 1947) Nevertheless, the *Empire Windrush* was to become the recognised historical landmark influencing successive waves of mass Caribbean migration initiatives to UK soil.

Women boarded on the Windrush were said to be a miniscule minority group. Lewis and Young (1998) identify the number of Caribbean women on board the Windrush in 1948 as officially totalling twelve. It is likely to assume that some are now deceased (Lewis and Young 1998; James and Harris 1993).

Initially, the majority of the Caribbean people intended for their travel to the United Kingdom to be temporary. For most, the original plan was to save enough money and eventually return to the Caribbean. In an abundance of cases, this did not work out to plan and UK residency became permanent (Bushnell and Warren 2010).

The term "Caribbean" is used to refer to all people of colour of Caribbean descent displaced following the migration process, who established and integrated with British nationals from the *Windrush* era onward. The *Windrush* period following the Second World War gave way to a surge in the migrant Caribbean population within British society. This influx would grow to form what would come to represent a multicultural society in Britain (Bushnell and Warren 2010).

Windrush was supposed to provide an opportunity for attaining financial mobility and contribute to the mother country because Caribbeans were deemed to be British colonial subjects. Many Caribbean men and women migrating to the United Kingdom would have been inspired by a lack of employment opportunities available in the Caribbean. Post-war Jamaica in 1945 was marked by a changing economic power base and a new order of racial stratification. Rural-based farming had become increasingly unprofitable due to export agriculture drying up.

Sugar production in the Caribbean, although still an important economic staple, had been increasingly diminishing. Sugar cane cultivation was considerably reduced between 1956 and 1965 in Antigua, Grenada, and in St Kitts, Nevis, and Anguilla. It was discarded in St Vincent in 1962 and in St Lucia in 1964. Many of the British Caribbean Islands were affected; Montserrat's smaller land space for sugar cultivation meant they were only using sugar cane to make rum and syrup. And in Trinidad and Jamaica, the industry's future was also in the balance (Dookhan 1975: 37–39).

After the war, as trade relations stabilised, sugar and rum returned to being in high demand in the United Kingdom. Unfortunately, owing to the post-WWII aftermath, there was a lack of shipping facilities, which meant that the British West Indian sugar industry was left seriously depleted (Dookhan 1975: 37, 38).

The ship-building industry was susceptible to an extreme rise and fall in output and employment. In England during 1955, an excess of one and a half million gross tons of shipping was over fifty years old. And at one point, there were incidents where new boilers were being fitted to ships constructed sixty years earlier. The general life span of dry cargo ships was thirty years. However, replacement was often postponed and only carried out when severe corrosion deemed the ship unrepairable.

From 1945 to 1957, "the demand for shipping exceeded supply … and supply of new ships remained virtually stationary" (Johnson, Whyman, Wykes 1968: 62, 64, 65). In addition to this, machinery in the Caribbean was in much need of modernisation. There was a lack of investment in the sugar-industry mechanisms as it became economically unrealistic. There was a likely risk of unemployment as the production of sugar in the Caribbean came at greater cost to small producers, who were not positioned well enough in the market to rival more efficient sugar-producing countries. This would have a serious effect on the economies of Trinidad, Guyana, Barbados, and Jamaica, for whom it was a source of government revenue, exports, and a financial lifeline for the substantial number of peasant farmers who grew sugar cane as a cash crop to sell to local factories (Dookhan 1975: 38, 39).

This dilemma initiated a push towards diversification of labour in order to source other methods of stimulating economic growth in the Caribbean region with a goal being to help raise the living standards and conditions of the working-class masses. Aside from agriculture, the search leaned towards developments in, "forestry, mining, livestock rearing, small scale manufacturing and tourism" (Dookhan 1975: 37–39).

However, forward-thinking ideas and strategies for diversification in the British Caribbean was in its infancy and still under construction. In the case of Jamaica, the ensuing poverty caused by the lack of opportunity led to a mass exodus of working-class blacks to seek employment opportunities in Kingston, Jamaica's urban centre. When there proved to be limited work available for the rural-based blacks, many began to seek employment opportunities in the mother country.

There was a similar situation in and amongst the other British West Indian Islands, that would require a unified approach with all the islands' combined efforts to effect positive changes for the future development of the region.

Caribbeans assumed a misguided notion of belonging, since bearing the title of colonial subject. A high proportion of Caribbeans envisaged coming to the United Kingdom as a prime opportunity for self-improvement (Lewis and Bryan 1991). Caribbean men and women were invited to the United Kingdom to help fill the gap in Britain's labour shortage after the Second World War (Phillips 2011).

The British Nationality Act of 1948 made British colonial subjects eligible to claim British citizenship, which allowed Caribbeans' rightful entry to live in Britain without the necessity of a visa (Karatani 2003; Bushnell and Warren 2010; Fryer 1984). The act of 1948 bestowed British citizenship on all Commonwealth subjects. In fact,

> Their passports literally documented their status as citizens of the United Kingdom and Colonies—(CUKC) engendered by the Act of 1948 consisted of all those British subjects who had a close relationship (either through birth or descent) with the United Kingdom and its remaining colonies. (Murdoch 2012: 82, 83) Also refer to appendix three: (Interviewee 1).

Despite this, the reception of Caribbean migrants by British host residents proved to be disappointingly unwelcoming. On countless occasions, as Phillips (1998) describes, "blatantly hostile".

According to Phillips, the statuses of the newly migrated Caribbean subjects, owing to the direct UK-colonial work recruitment programmes, were purposefully initiated to facilitate Caribbeans' role as a replacement labour population. Examples of this will be explored. London Transport officials travelled to Barbados to set up office in 1954 for the purpose of recruiting staff to work on UK buses and trains. Other recruitment campaigns came in the form of seeking workers for the National Health Service; it was still in its early inception, having commenced in 1948. Coupled with this in the northern regions of the United Kingdom, textile companies recruited workers from India and Pakistan (Bushnell and Warren 2010: 5).

Initiatives such as these would serve to incentivize mass migration. This would likely have been underpinned by the notion of being able to gain economic stability and the accumulation of wealth once willing to work and strive for it and in line with the ideological conditions of their migration to the United Kingdom. For instance, concerning London Transport, the Commonwealth governments were largely in support of the work programmes in England. Some offered interest-free travel loans to encourage the uptake. And on arrival to the United Kingdom, London Transport provided hostel accommodations for its workers.

The post–World War II labour force was mainly outsourced from chosen regions of the British West Indies, India, and Pakistan (Phillips 1998: 1682–1683). The perceptions of the indigenous population to those of the new arrivals were diametrically opposed, giving rise to a negative response and, in turn, conflict.

On arrival, Caribbeans initially tended to settle in the deprived inner-city metropolises such as Brixton South London, Handsworth-Birmingham, and Toxteth in Liverpool (Bushnell and Warren 2010; Barn 2001). Overall, the Caribbean *Windrush* entrants were skilled workers, but the jobs available to Caribbean people were mainly for unskilled, toiling work (Carter 1987).

Approximately half of the arrivals already had accommodations in place.

The remainder were temporarily housed in an air-raid shelter in Clapham, South London. The closest employment exchange was situated in Brixton.

Due to this, Brixton became a settlement hub for many Caribbeans arriving in London city centre. (Patterson 1965; Phillips and Phillips 1999).

Metropolitan-based concentrations of Caribbean migrants led to social discord in many regions, London being no exception. This prompted the government to act in order to be seen as taking control of the situation. Actions included a prelude to the implementation of the 1962 Commonwealth Immigrants Act and alleviating the English host anxieties over the Caribbean migrant influx (Sivanandan 1982).

1.2 Aim and Objectives

Aim

- To locate and document the *Windrush*-era housing experiences of eight Caribbean women, commencing with their arrival in the United Kingdom and continuously charting their housing experiences until 2014.

Objectives:

- To identify Caribbean women's published literature of *Windrush* experiences (1948–1970).

- To discuss Caribbeans' struggles, notably with regards to a lack of access to decent housing provision.

- To examine and acknowledge Caribbeans' ability to adopt self-help measures to acquire their housing goals.

Figure 4: Caribbean Migrant Arrival in the United Kingdom

Newly arrived Caribbean migrants coming in at Victoria Station,
London, after their journey from Southampton Docks.

Source: Hulton Getty Archive. *Picture Post* (published 1956). Photo by Haywood Magee.

CHAPTER 2

Literature Review

This literature review covers literature relating to race, ethnicity, and housing. There has been found to be a fair amount of literature both within the United Kingdom and the United States based on:

- Discrimination in housing markets, especially regarding access of black and ethnic minority communities to housing. Also, in reference to discrimination in access to council housing and mortgage approval by Caribbean men and women during the 1960s and 1970s. Two of the earliest studies highlighting the issues facing Caribbeans during the migration phase are Patterson (1965) and Rex and Moore (1967) in their studies of Sparkbrook. These literatures highlight discriminatory practices by borough councils and housing policy.

- Taking a broader view and differing literary perspectives, reference is made to examples of ethnic segregation of cities and poor city neighbourhoods in continuing to assess the causes of deprived and marginalised inner-city areas within the United Kingdom and the United States. These include Peach (1998), Phillips and Harrison (2010), Massey and Denton (2010), Wilson (2010) cited in Bridge and Watson, and Wacquant (2008).

- Publications by Caribbean women of the *Windrush* migration experience and settlement in the United Kingdom have proved to be non-existent. It appears that black literature relating to this period did not emerge until decades later. However, the life of Caribbean novelist and schoolteacher Beryl Gilroy, who was resident in the United Kingdom at the time of *Windrush* but whose aspirations were not able to be expressed until some substantial years later, will be drawn on in the review.

2.1 Identifying Patterns of Migration and Settlement Struggles through Extracts from Post-War Narratives

The aim of the following section is to try to impart some sense of black identity through a taster of Caribbean literature, poetry, and creative writing relating to the post-war *Windrush* migration and settlement struggles of Caribbean women and men.

The dismantling of the British Empire coincided with decolonisation, commencing with West Indian independence in Jamaica and Trinidad and Tobago, who became independent nation states in 1962 (Alleyne 2002), drawing reference to what Louise Bennett-Coverley, also fondly known as 'Miss Lou' Jamaican folklore poet, author and playwright, aptly describes as, "colonisation in reverse" (Burnett 1986). The surge of Caribbean migration in the late 1940s, 1950s, and 1960s could be construed as contributing to Britain's prevailing image of destabilisation as an empire, along with its firm patriotism as a monoculture society, that was now changing and being challenged due to the rising multicultural population, particularly in London, aside from other metropolitan city centres (Jones, cited in Owusu 2000: 49).

During the post–World War II period, a fair number of writers and artists came to reside in England from the Caribbean. The BBC's Caribbean Voices Programme afforded them the opportunity to network and become acquainted with each other's work. This inspired the formation of the Caribbean Artists Movement (CAM), in 1966. (Alleyne 2002: 32, 33; Donnell and Lawson Welsh 1996: 214, 215).

Beryl Gilroy, a pioneering novelist and schoolteacher, was born in Guyana in 1924 and came to Britain in 1951. As a black woman she found herself faced with discrimination which prevented her in the early years from obtaining work as a teacher. Gilroy decided to improve her career prospects by attending the University of London from 1951 until 1953, where she studied child development. Gilroy's sources of employment include factory work, washing dishes at Lyons and domestic work (Peepaltree Press 2014). In 1959, Gilroy wrote her first novel, *In Praise of Love and Children*, but she was unable to secure a publisher until 1994. Despite the existence of the CAM, Gilroy would testify in her autobiography, *Black Teacher* (1976; 1994), and as stressed by Courtman (2012), the, "invisibility of women of the Windrush generation", black writers of Caribbean literature was male dominated.

Caribbean Voices commenced in 1943 and operated until 1958. It was set up originally to broadcast poems and stories as well as current affairs back to the Caribbean, allowing separated Caribbean servicemen to maintain a link with family. This valuable broadcast served as a magnet in attracting new male Caribbean writers to Britain, many of whom went on to be published (Courtman 2014). However, it would seem, stemming from the void in women's discourse, that these same opportunities were not afforded to Caribbean female writers at that time (Courtman 2014).

Gilroy got married, an interracial union, and would become one of the first black head teachers in the United Kingdom. Throughout the high and low points in Gilroy's teaching career, the one constant that kept her going was her love of teaching and the children; although the internal politics and dynamics of the school setting was rapidly changing at that time. Along with a fading British empirical structure, saw schools having to admit children from different countries and cultures, which was hard for many White British-born teachers to adapt to and caused much resentment that frequently got vented inappropriately and directly at Black, Asian and (to a lesser extent) children from other European minority countries. (Gilroy, 1994: 148, 149, 150). Gilroy would skilfully address these feelings in open discussion, by way of initiating staff group therapy sessions. Although Gilroy admits in the teaching profession her love of her job was always being tested by the difficulty of just being accepted for who she was, a black woman:

> My life at school was clouded by an obsessive interest in my 'blackness'. It seemed that no one could forget it, and no one really wanted *me* to forget it … It was difficult, at times, not to become the traditional black with the traditional chip on the shoulder. (Gilroy, 1994: 62)

It seems that Beryl Gilroy's relative obscurity throughout the Windrush phase (1948–1970) was likely due to her being a product of her generation, when women had less rights accorded to them (Courtman 2014; Peepaltree Press 2014). Sivanandan (1982) speaks of Caribbeans' and Asians' inabilities to fathom the petty prejudice, that was not exclusive to housing and employment, visible from the English host society (Sivanandan 1982: 5).

Caribbeans would develop their own places to network socially, such as barbershops and cafes, as well as hanging out on street corners. These congregation hotspots mirrored familiar behaviour patterns present back home in the Caribbean (Sivanandan 1982: 5, 6; McLeod 2004: 1, 2).

In Sheila Patterson's study of Caribbeans in Brixton in her book, Dark Strangers (1965), that she conducted in May 1955, she appears slightly mesmerised by the sizeable concentration of Caribbean men and women in Brixton, where she observed them socialising, roaming, and hanging out—or "liming"—on the streets (Selvon, 1956: 100, 105, 114), and generally going about their daily affairs. Patterson observes not only their behaviours but their clothing, namely the Caribbean men's lightweight suits, distinctive because of the baggy cut and testimony to their new arrival in the United Kingdom (Patterson 1965: 13).

Patterson recalls images of the men queuing outside the employment agency, adamant to get on and make a life for themselves. Patterson's gaze moves on to a nursery situated within the vicinity, which she refers to as post-war prefabricated houses/buildings made of asbestos-cement, discernible for their quick and cheap assembly. Built between 1946 and 1948, this was a short-term measure to help combat the housing crisis (Patterson 1965: 13; Johnson, Whyman, and Wykes 1968: 72).

Patterson's interesting depiction of the nursery children's varying shades of black is drawn upon. She describes them as *café noir* or *café au lait* in colouring (Patterson, 1965: 13). This drew attention to the hybridity of mixed ethnicity following the intermixing of black and white, serving as an indication of changing times or tokenisms of cultural integration. (Patterson 1965: 13; McLeod 2004: 1, 2) The change reflected the contradictions and complexities of a changing landscape, where Caribbean immigrants seek adoption by the mother country while carving their imprint, forever changing the complexion of English society.

Cobham and Collins (Agard, cited in Cobham and Collins (eds) 1987: 89, 90) have compiled a poignant array of creative writings by black women in Britain. An extract of Agard's poem "A House", was selected because it strikes a familiar chord and picks up on themes expressed by the women in this case study, characterising the housing situation experienced by Caribbean women—and men and children—in Britain during the 1950s and 1960s, although interestingly retold through a little girl's eyes.

Agard's poem captures the experiences of communal living amongst families compacted into overcrowded lodging houses. It would be unthinkable now to have a kitchen situated on the landing due to likely health and safety risks. However, these circumstances were tolerated and even normalised in the period of Caribbean post-war settlement. The Dutch pot is a heavy, iron, bowl-shaped cooking pot Caribbeans commonly used (and still use) for cooking traditional Caribbean meals, such as stewed chicken.

The poem identifies the racism within educational institutions that Caribbean children were often subjected to. The issue of childcare posed a very real issue for Caribbean women. Coming from extended family networks which facilitate the reliance on mothers, sisters, aunts, and grandmothers. Rex and Moore acknowledge the plight of Caribbean women in their study: "They lack the extensive, dense kinship network of their home. Crucially for the women, this deprives them of aid in caring for children" (Rex and Moore, 1967: 114).

Due to a combination of unsympathetic landlords, coupled with childcare issues, and other factors, women sometimes sent their children back to the Caribbean for periods in order to relieve the pressure. (See chapter 4, interviewees 5, 7, and 8).

A House

A House full of loud noises, Rich smells,
    painful tears and side-splitting laughter.
A House in which three families lived
    tightly squeezed together
We were right at the top.

There were two rooms;
A bedroom and a living room;
    with the kitchen on the landing
On which the heavy iron stove
    with its black dutch pots
    stood in all its splendid glory

A House of running feet
On uncarpeted polished stairs;
I slipped once
    and broke my shoulder
    after being warned.
I attended school my arm in a sling
    when the teacher was having
    us act out some nursery rhymes.
Guess who was a blackbird
    sling and all.

I remember flapping my good arm-wing
For I was dressed for the part.
I was praised most highly for my efforts
    broken shoulder and all!
We did a lot of play-acting.
I have always hated that
    nursery rhyme and blackbirds.
Before broken shoulders
    and hateful nursery rhymes
    there were the tears of my mother
    as she was forced to leave me
    with yet another nanny.

This is a story that was often
    told in that House ...

Sandra Agard

2.2 Housing Policy and Tenure in Post-WWII Britain

To give a clearer understanding of the housing situation in post-WWII Britain, housing policies implemented to facilitate property development are explored in order to show the shaping of housing strategies and the thinking behind tenure expansion and improvement.

Post-war housing policy commenced with the implementation of the 1947 Town and Country Planning Act, that delegated power to local authorities to obtain land under the direction of Aneurin Bevan. The depletion of housing stock was severe. The WWII bombings had taken their toll, leaving approximately 450,000 properties destroyed or structurally unliveable. In particular, more affordable housing was necessary to meet the needs of the underprivileged (Lowe 2011: 85; Lund 2011: 53).

Homeownership became more favourable beginning in 1938. Prior to this, private landlord rental tenures dominated the housing market at approximately 57 per cent (Lund 2011: 51). The end of WWII in 1945 saw Aneurin Bevan appointed in charge of the housing programme.

The government extended a generous flat rate subsidy for "general needs" houses. The subsidy was improved by triple the amount supplemented during the 1930s (Lund 2011, 53). Bevan stipulated local authorities be compelled to make a rateable contribution to property construction. These local authorities were permitted to lend from the Public Works Loans Board below the market rate. Coupled with this, a strict building licence system to monitor the use of materials by the private sector was imposed.

Local-authority properties were planned to form an integrated part of the urban landscape, an initiative to stimulate mixed-community environments that incorporated an assortment of home occupancy types. The 1949 Housing Act removed the clause disallowing middle-class access to occupying social housing (Lund 2011: 54; Lowe 2011: 86).

Poor housing conditions were exposed in the 1951 census. A high proportion of properties across England, Scotland, and Wales were found to be without basic amenities, such as a fixed bath, piped hot running water, a water closet, or a cooking stove (Lund 2011: 55).

Bevan held the view that local authorities should become the pioneers of house building as they were better positioned to meet the needs of people facing poverty in order to provide homes with affordable rents. Bevan's prefabricated bungalows building programme, activated in 1944, was terminated in 1948 as a review of the properties deemed them to be of inferior quality with restricted space. Bevan sought to provide better quality housing than what had been erected during the interwar period, as well as providing larger dwelling space, with an extra 134 square feet added. The properties had upstairs and downstairs living quarters, outbuildings, and water closets.

For the shorter term, the focus was to be firmly fixed on those in the direst need. As such, local authorities placed priority on building houses for rental purposes rather than building mortgaged properties. This was reflected in Labour's 1951 manifesto (Lund 2011: 54).

During the 1951 Conservative Party election campaign, a declaration pledged to increase public and private property building to 300,000 per year. This inevitably swayed voters, leading to a conservative victory.

In 1953, under Minister for Housing Harold Macmillan, 300,000 properties were built. Out of this figure, 245,000 were erected by local authorities (Lowe 2011: 85, 90; Lund 2011: 55, 56). According to Lee (1994), under the Macmillan government, initially, the houses built for owner occupancy at 15 per cent, increased to 63 per cent in 1963. In 1964, there were continued demands for an increase in property development due to a combination of slum clearance and increased marriages coupled with escalating birth rates (Lee, cited in Jones [eds] 1994: 210).

During WWII, according to the economic and social historical findings of Johnson, Whyman, and Wykes:

Half of the million workers in the building industry were conscripted into the armed forces. Those remaining were mainly engaged in constructing military camps, aerodromes and hospitals, together with house repair work. All new building had to be licensed by the government, and private building virtually ceased. (Johnson, Whyman, and Wykes 1968: 71)

After the war, there was a mammoth task of meeting the backlog against the desperate public outcry to replace housing that was no longer fit for purpose and repair those that were salvageable. This was in addition to overcoming the issue of shortages of labour and building materials.

The Labour government saw fit to make use of empty office blocks. Controls would be re-exerted pertaining to building standards and an aim established to impose fair rents and rent rebates, as well as for the land commission to hasten house building. With the swelling population, apart from the need for houses, there was also an increasing demand for schools, factories, offices, and shops in highly depleted areas (Johnson, Whyman, and Wykes 1968: 71).

Pressure groups urged the government to act in order to be seen as taking control of the housing crisis. There was increasing awareness of the housing shortage, coupled with chronic poverty, that showed a less glamorous side to the so-called swinging sixties, especially in light of documented programmes such as *Cathy Come Home*, a documentary focusing on the deprivation of the homeless that was first aired on television in 1966. The programme unearthed the story of young couple Cathy and Reg, who faced the plight of homelessness. Coupled with disagreements arising from which of them should assume responsibility for the children, whilst being jostled between local authorities. Cathy and her children ended up in a dilapidated dormitory, which excluded her partner Reg. It would lead to the relationship breaking down and sadly the local authority would take the children into care. The programme reflected the experiences of numerous homeless people during the 1950s and 60s. (Lund 2011: 160; Lund 2016: 216)

In 1967, the housing charity Shelter was established and entrusted Nick Hedges with the special task of travelling around the country photographing shockingly substandard housing conditions throughout England and Wales (Bushnell and Warren 2010: 56; Geoff Lee, cited in Jones (eds) 1994.

Figure 5 shows the changing pattern of tenure in Britain over the last century, commencing in 1918 through to 2011 ONS census statistical information.

Figure 5: Home Ownership and Rentals, 1918–2011

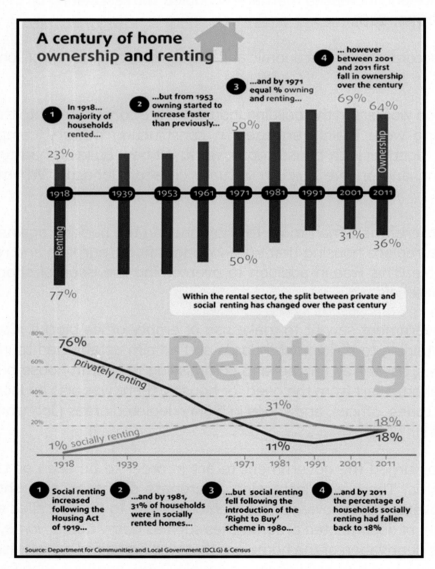

Source: Courtesy of the ONS; data from the Office for National Statistics licensed under the Open Government Licence V.3.0.

2.3 The Caribbean Migrant Housing Experience

The objective of the emerging section commences with identifying the housing experiences of Caribbean migrants during the early part of their residency and settlement in London. Also, the changing patterns of tenure by Caribbean and White households in London will be explored focusing on 1991 and 2011 census statistics. Followed by the development of Black Minority Ethnic housing associations; then turning the focus to how British urban cities are racialised. Lastly, the matter of choice versus constraint will be assessed pertaining to continued black concentration within metropolitan city regions.

Discrimination in housing has been identified as a problem, especially in the private sector. Mullard asserts that discrimination in housing operated on various levels:

"Local authority, individual landlord, and at the level where landlords would accept black tenants—but only at a price" (Mullard 1973: 42).

With reference to council housing, discrimination likely was exercised covertly, as indicated by Rex and Moore (1967: 24–27) in their study of Sparkbrook in Birmingham. Under Birmingham Council's policy, newly arrived Caribbeans were essentially off limits when it came to being considered for council housing as they would need to have lived and worked within Birmingham's metropolitan region for at least five years before qualifying for the waiting list. Following this, the Caribbean applicant would still have needed to move up the priority category for housing by way of a points system. So finally, after waiting five years to get on the housing list, they could only move up the housing allocations ladder by accumulating points (Rex and Moore 1967: 24).

Similar protocols pertaining to council access probably existed in most borough councils. In the case of Lambeth Council, according to Patterson (1965: 157–159), the borough council's property waiting list contained the applications of approximately 10,000 families in January 1955. This, she documented, was some months prior to beginning her study of Caribbeans living within the vicinity of Brixton. They had to wait three years before qualifying as a borough resident in order to make an application to go on the housing list. Patterson voices that "No significant number of coloured families could have qualified even for entry on the waiting-list until 1957, when rehousing practically ceased" (Patterson 1965: 157-8). Gross overcrowding was voiced by Patterson to be of common knowledge in 1955 for Caribbean immigrants and it had been said by informants that, "applications for re-housing from coloured families were often marked and therefore distinguishable when they went up before the Housing Committee for consideration." (Ibid: 158) It is unsurprising that Patterson would add that this claim was officially denied.

Caribbeans had to be grateful for whatever they could get (Barn 2001: 9; Fryer 1984: 383), even if rundown, dilapidated, or infested. It was common practice for two, three, or even four or more persons to share a room (Selvon 1990: 18). Sometimes Caribbeans who didn't even know each other were forced to share the same bed (see chapter 4, "Interviewee 1"; Phillips and Phillips 1999: 89–92).

It has been said that racially divisive policies ensured that council properties were not an option available to the Caribbean immigrant who was not eligible, often due to ignorance of the housing system, lack of resources, and discrimination (Harrison 1998: 798; Phillips and Harrison 2010: 222; Hamnett and Butler 2010: 57).

Bernie Grant, in his thirteen-year post as Haringey Borough Council (Labour) constituency MP, actively engaged with black and ethnic minorities, indeed all marginalised groups within his constituency. He observed from within government biased housing policies that marginalised Caribbean migrants. MP Bernie Grant spoke of his experiences and on housing policy. He openly spoke about the difficulty black people faced, in securing private rental properties and the familiar signs on English properties; signs boldly displayed, that stated *no Blacks, no Irish, no dogs, no Children.* (Bushnell and Warren, 2010;12)

In addition to hidden institutional racism disguised in policies connected to government run organisations, such as in housing and in education. He discussed as was shown by Patterson (1965), that newly arrived Caribbeans needed to have borough connections, by way of the three-year residency rule as well as family living there stemming over three generations, to which Mr Grant expressed as 'moving the goalposts.' He concluded that due to these frequent predicaments faced by Caribbeans he became actively involved with a considerable amount of anti-racist work. (Ibid: 12)

Caribbeans were left with limited housing options other than to rent from fellow Caribbean, Patterson, 1965: 55; refers to … *"a small group of 'old-timer' black landlords settled in Brixton, whose properties were to form the nuclei of the future settlement"* … or Jewish people, as was often the case. As discussed earlier, many English people were often said to have exhibited notices rejecting Blacks, Irish, or dogs (Carter 1987: 30, 31). Most of the case-study women recall seeing such postings when they arrived in the United Kingdom. Patterson also emphasizes that in her Brixton based Caribbean study, she identified that apart from Caribbean and Jewish landlords, other non-English 'boarding house or rooming-house proprietors' (Patterson, 1965: 55) willing to rent to Caribbeans, were an increasing number of former immigrants since the war:

> Southern Irish, Polish, or Cypriot; and some of these seem to have had less colour consciousness, and to have been rather more willing than the local land-ladies to accept coloured lodgers. (Patterson, 1965: 55)

Following the women's case-study research conducted for this book, it was revealed that migrants who arrived between 1948 and 1950 were compelled to rent from English landlords as established Caribbean proprietors were practically non-existent.

As the migrant influx escalated, host sentiments became more embittered. Despite the fact of Caribbeans' low wages (Phillips 1998), they aspired to the goal of home ownership (Phillips and Phillips 1999: 132) fuelled by the desire to gain more stability for themselves and their families. St-Jean Kufour (2000) states that by 1974, Caribbeans mortgaged tenure acquisition was on par with English homeowners.

However, commencing from the 1980s, these statistics would take a nosedive, with English homeownership figures at approximately 65 per cent, compared to Caribbeans' at 46 per cent. It has been asserted that this correlates with Caribbeans gaining access to council dwellings (St-Jean Kufour, cited in Owusu 2000: 328).

Customised data (table 1) of the 1991 census local base statistics has been collated from Nomis, (originally conducted on 29 March 2014) and revised in September 2022, that show statistics for white and black households in the London metropolitan region. In 1991, the total black Caribbeans' household tenure figure stood at 125,253, compared to the white total household figure of 2,337,489.

The figures for black Caribbean households renting from local authorities were 48,901 and from housing associations 13,107, which would seem to coincide with St Jean Kufour's (2000) analysis, stated earlier, that commencing from the eighties, Caribbeans' mortgaged house purchasing levels dropped with the upward trend of accessing local authority tenure.

Table 1. Tenure by Ethnicity of Household, London, 1991 ONS Census – Local base Statistics

Dataset: (TABLE 1)	1991 Census - local base statistics	
Source:	ONS Crown Copyright Reserved [from Nomis on September 7 2022]	
	Regions	
Area Name:	**London**	
Date:	**1991**	

Table L49 Ethnic Group; housing: Households with residents; residents in households [100%]

(Dorrel Green-Briggs) 1991 Census - Local base Statistics for London Region

Adapted: 8 September 2022

		Ethnic group of household head	
	TOTAL HOUSEHOLDS	White	Black Caribbean
ALL HOUSEHOLDS	2,763,166	2,337,489	125,253
Over 1 and up to 1.5 ppr	75,706	39,858	4,947
Over 1.5 ppr	38,162	19,632	2,192
Owner occupied - owned outright	492,145	459,308	8,568
Owner occupied - buying	1,088,321	904,953	46,789
Rented privately	338,200	289,762	6,721
Rented from a housing association	154,711	122,486	13,107
Rented from a LA or new town	644,861	522,666	48,901
Lacking or sharing use of bath/shower and/ or inside WC	65,917	54,508	2,032
No central heating	518,931	464,843	18,536

ppr = persons per room

ONS: Adapted from data from the Office for National Statistics licensed under the Open Government Licence V.3.0.

Source: Courtesy of the ONS; adapted from data from the Office for National Statistics licensed under the Open Government Licence V.3.0.

The 1991 census findings show Caribbean household owner-occupants buying their homes at 46,789. Caribbeans living in local authority household figures is higher, 48,901. More revealingly, the figures for black Caribbean outright owner-occupants were a mere 8,568. Poor housing conditions often leads to increased health issues (Nazroo, cited in Owusu 2000: 315) In 1991, Caribbean households without central heating stood at 18,536, which was very high in relation to the total Caribbean households of 125,253. White households without central heating were considerably lower at 464,843 when comparing the total white household figure of 2,337,489.

The total Caribbean household's tenure figure, 163,636, highlighted in table 2, is part of the total black British households' population figure, amounting to 416,365 in the London region.

In contrast, table 2 reveals the 2011 ONS census local base statistics (originally collated in 2014, from Nomis and revised in September 2022) established that the total black Caribbean household of all tenure figures have risen to 163, 636; a rise of 38,383 for Caribbeans living in London. However, the total white household tenure figure for 2011 in London was 2,183,640, which shows a decline since the 1991 statistics, of white households living in London by 153,849. This maybe an indicator of white concentrations in London thinning out and that white households favour moving to the suburbs and rural areas (Macewen, 1991: 161), while Caribbean households become more concentrated within particular London areas as in other inner-city metropolitan regions.

A mini survey was completed in 2014, titled *The Housing Experiences and Aspirations of Black British-Caribbeans Living in London* by twenty-three affiliate Caribbean neighbourhood community residents living in North London. Although this is a small sample, participants responses are notable in showing that most expressed a desire or preference to live in areas that reflect a multiracial mix. Some survey candidates also expressed uncertainty, fear, or vulnerability of living in areas lacking cultural diversity. In 2011, black Caribbeans outright owner-occupants in London were 20,222, a growth of 11,654 since 1991 census figures.

The numbers of Caribbean household owner-occupants with a mortgage/or buying through shared ownership fell slightly in 2011 to 46,449, compared to 1991 figures of 46,789 (a decrease of 340 households). Caribbean households residing in local authority tenure fell to 39,365 in 2011, a reduction of 9,536 from the previous figure in 1991 of 48,901. Housing association and other social rented Caribbean household figures rose according to 2011 census findings to 34,969 from just 13,107 in 1991. Finally, the number of Caribbean households renting from private landlords or letting agencies has risen to 20,202, an increase of 13,481 since 1991.

Table 2. Tenure by Ethnicity of Household, London, 2011 ONS Census – Local base Statistics

DC4201EW: (TABLE 2) – Tenure by Ethnic Group – Household Reference Persons

ONS Crown Copyright Reserved [from Nomis on 7 September 2022]

Adapted: 8 September 2022

(Dorrel Green-Briggs) 2011 Census - Local base Statistics for London Region

population	All Household Reference Persons
Units:	Household reference persons
Date:	2011
Area type:	regions
Area name:	London
Age:	All categories: Age

Ethnic Group	All categories: Tenure	Owned or shared ownership: Total	Owned: Owned outright	Owned: Owned with a mortgage; loan or shared ownership	Social rented: Total	Social rented: Rented from council Local (Authority)	Social rented: Other social rented	Private rented or living rent free: Total	Private rented: Private landlord or letting agency	Private rented: Other private rented or living rent free
All categories: Ethnic group	3,266,173	1,618,315	689,898	928,417	785,993	439,727	346,266	861,865	775,591	86,274
White: Total	2,183,640	1,190,495	555,435	635,060	441,815	248,228	193,587	551,330	496,781	54,549
White: English/Welsh/Scottish/Northern Irish/British	1,664,434	997,191	476,460	520,731	355,101	200,094	155,007	312,142	272,550	39,592
Black/African/Caribbean/Black British: Total	416,365	126,287	30,705	95,582	198,232	110,559	87,673	91,846	82,631	9,215
Black/African/Caribbean/Black British: Caribbean	163,636	66,671	20,222	46,449	74,334	39,365	34,969	22,631	20,202	2,429

In order to protect against disclosure of personal information, records have been swapped between different geographic areas. Some counts will be affected, particularly small counts at the lowest geographies. Private rented: Other private rented or living rent free' includes the groups 'Private rented: Other' and 'Living rent free'. 'Owned: Owned with a mortgage or loan or shared ownership' includes 'Owned: Owned with a mortgage or loan' and 'Shared ownership (part owned and part rented)'.

Source: Courtesy of the ONS; adapted from data from the Office for National Statistics licensed under the Open Government Licence V.3.0.

The Development of Black Minority Ethnic (BME) Housing Associations

As far as progress in housing provision goes relating to black marginalised communities, following on from the 1980s, Brian Lund (2016) assesses how diversity and equality would become part of the housing policy agenda following the race riots of the 1980s. The 1981 and 1985 backlash led to further investigation by the Home Office researchers that linked the upheaval with socio-economic factors:

> Intrinsic factors may include forms of social deprivation and disadvantage (Benyon 1986: 18)

Reports such as John Benyon's (1986) amongst others, (Institute of Race Relations, 1987: 2; Solomos, 1993: 138) would contribute to heightening awareness of racialised social deprivation and disadvantage combined with The Commission for Racial Equality, that revealed racial discrimination within housing. By way of providers' service activities, negatively impacting minority and marginalised groups. (Lund 2016: 193) In response to these findings and in addition to increased organised local community-based anti-racist campaigns for improved access to housing; stimulated the additional development of housing associations to facilitate diversity to allay the situation. Lund locates how the foregoing findings caused The Housing Corporation to formulate its Black and Minority Ethnic (BME) Housing Policy with the aim being to promote BME associations to support the housing needs and necessities of minority communities, and committed to steering resources to improve disadvantaged neighbourhoods, whilst also seeking to promote black leadership. Owing to the BME Housing Policy and ventures, would help to stimulate the growth of over sixty BME housing associations. (Lund 2016: 193)

How British Urban Cities are Racialised

David Sibley's journalistic discourse entitled *'The racialisation of space in British cities'* discusses the psychological impact of how real and imaginary geographical city spaces are racialised (Sibley, cited in Lewis and Young, eds, 1998: 122). Sibley uses the example of Richard Dyer's discourse on film and representation showing how in films set in Africa between the 1930s to the 1960s made comparisons between a 'restrained and orderly colonial society and black mobs.' (Ibid: 122) This depiction of two extreme elements of imagery that linked 'whiteness' as being associated with efficiency and reasoned actions whilst 'blackness' on the other hand visually represented an imagery of unruliness and irrationality. Sibley uses these depictions to draw parallels to:

> Racist portrayals of British inner cities with substantial African-Caribbean populations. Racialised white suburban spaces could be characterised in one stereotypical view of the city as ordered, homogeneous and pure, a circle of virtue enclosing inner areas of deviance and disorder. (Sibley, cited in Lewis and Young, eds, 1998: 122)

Sibley states that stereotypes have been mainly used when referring to people, although he confers that the 'material world' can also function to objectify people linked to places through the psychological tarnish of imagery. Where spatial areas can come to be labelled as good or bad such as the 'black inner city' by showing compelling images of negative and positive or good and bad in people and the built environment in which they reside in, encapsulating an occurrence in a particular historical time-frame that can be recalled to memory. The media portrayals and representations have served to home in on inner-city disturbances, resistance and retaliations occurring during the 1980s visually that psychologically resonate with past depictions of:

> Colonised peoples and places. Places like Brixton and Toxteth were represented as disordered landscapes. (Ibid: 121; Solomos, 1993: 137)

Sibley further highlights the perceived threat of the invasion of the inner-city landscape and views shared by colonial administrators in Africa and India, in the past imagery that fed into the wider perceptions of a more prevailing unrest, and the threat of some 'other' breaching its spatial boundaries. A striking portrayal is used when Sibley draws on Paul Hoggett's reference to:

> The symbolic importance of the cockroach in white racist representations of the Bangladeshi population in London's east end, the cockroach conveying both an abject other, through elision with the radicalised minority, but also one which threatened to invade the secure spaces of the white population. (Sibley, cited in Lewis and Young, eds, 1998: 121)

The final example that will be used from Sibley's insightful discourse inter-played with the visual technology of imagery; that would give a worldwide platform and exposure to the beating of Rodney King, in America, 1991. Where a black man driving his car in a white suburb was seen to be a threat to a contained, secure suburban 'white' space in Los Angeles, and a black man driving freely through, was to represent a threat of black infiltration and invasion. (Ibid: 121)

Choice versus constraint and BME Housing Concentration

Phillips and Harrison (2010: 223) state that researchers seeking to find answers for the black minority ethnic housing concentration, segregation, and deprivation continue to be compelled by issues of minority choice versus constraint.

Peach (1998: 1667, 1668) draws reference from the 1991 local base statistics to the higher concentrations of Caribbeans, in particular Jamaican migrants, geographically located in South London. Peach surmises that despite the fact constraints exist in terms of accessibility to sectors of the housing market, location can constitute a magnet for continued ethnic clustering and concentration (As conveyed earlier by Patterson 1965: 55) that can be construed as choice-based desirability to settle in one particular area over another.

Proceeding to draw on the possible causes of segregation within cities and marginality based on US discourse, Massey and Denton (cited in Bridge and Watson 2010: 177–183) attribute the persistency of segregation within US metropolitan areas ultimately to the fact of race. They persuasively show that despite the rise in socio-economic levels, the black population continues to be represented in highly segregated areas.

> White prejudice is such that when black entry into a neighbourhood is achieved, that area becomes unattractive to further white settlement and whites begin departing at an accelerated pace. This segmentation of black and white housing demand is encouraged by pervasive discrimination in the allocation of mortgages and home improvement loans, which systematically channel money away from integrated areas. (Massey and Denton, cited in Bridge and Watson 2010: 183)

However, in contrast, Wilson (cited in Bridge and Watson, 2010: 186, 187) takes the viewpoint that deindustrialised black urban cities which have become economically depressed by entrenched unemployment have become increasingly marginalised with working families moving out, thereby creating a haven for criminal activities and hopelessness, and in short, long-term economic collapse. Left behind, according to Wilson, are underclass ghetto neighbourhoods.

Waquant (2008: 2, 3, 4, 9) takes a multilayered approach as the factor contributing to segregation and marginalisation of the black American ghetto. According to Waquant, this stems from the urban unrest of the 1960s and what he describes as the combination of class, race, and state restructuring.

Returning to UK literature, Phillips and Harrison (2010) confer that settlement following the post-war period was, for Caribbeans, initially symbolised by housing deprivation concentrated in inner-city UK regions. These conditions were fuelled by racist discrimination that acted as a barrier to social housing access. Caribbeans were relegated to private renting at the low end of the private market as mortgaged finance was unobtainable due to limited income. In more recent years, there has been a reversal of this process, with Caribbean people prevalent in social housing, more so than Asian ethnic minority groups. Caribbean containment within inner-city areas has persisted to a considerable extent, although some de-concentration has occurred through the implementation of choice-based letting systems by some landlords. However, this can only be successful if accompanied, in the words of Phillips and Harrison, by, "well-resourced and proactive community-based anti-racist work …" although, "Tackling areas where minority populations are concentrated can do little to alter one causative factor of segregation; the locational choices exercised by better-off white households" (Phillips and Harrison 2010: 232).

Ultimately, in acknowledging the arguments put forward, Wacquant's (2008) perspective appears to be most relevant in the assessment that class, race, and state are all factors that impinge on the continued Caribbean containment and clustering within inner-city metropolitan regions and, therefore, likely act as contributory components in the persistence of marginalisation and segregation in UK urban cities.

2.4 Caribbean's Housing Aspirations and Self-Help Strategies

The final section in chapter 2 draws on the power of self-determinism and Caribbeans' ability to adapt and endure in challenging circumstances.

Caribbean settlement was a gradual process that only gained momentum since 1954 (Fryer 1984: 372). However, as the black presence became more prevalent, it stimulated more blatant outbursts of aggression from the English public fuelled by political propaganda and Sir Oswald Mosley's fascist union movement, the British Union of Fascists, that was formed in 1932.

Mosley was known to have ties with the Nazi Party, which later caused him to be deemed a threat to national security (Bushnell and Warren 2010: 10). Nevertheless, his influential position as a parliamentary candidate for the North Kensington constituency was to intensify the situation in the area. It peaked with the Notting Hill riots in 1958, followed by the murder of thirty-three-year-old Kelso Cochrane, an Antiguan carpenter, in May 1959 (Sivanandan 1982: 10; Phillips and Phillips 1999: 181, 182; Mullard 1973: 48). Kelso Cochrane was stabbed to death during the daytime; therefore, it was unlikely that no one witnessed any part of the attack. Sadly, no one came forward to give evidence of what transpired. There were more than 1,200 people in attendance at his funeral, and in 2009, precisely fifty years after his death, a blue plaque was placed at the spot where he was stabbed in honour of his memory and the impact the incident had on the black community and in improving community race relations in the Notting Hill area to make it a better place to live for future generations of Caribbeans living in the vicinity (Murdoch 2012: 97, 99). This tragedy would resonate strongly within the Caribbean community and even across the waters to the Caribbean region and in America, thereby uniting black political activism across the world.

Caribbeans living in the United Kingdom were able relate to and connect with the global struggle and speeches conveyed by high-profile figures like Martin Luther King Jr and Malcolm X as well as female pan-Africanists collective experiences globally for the right to racial equality. The year 1944 was to mark the founding of the British sector of the Pan-African Congress (PAC). They also maintained strong ties with local movements in the Caribbean, where the united struggles converged into a unified drive to secure democratic rights, civil liberties, and self-determinism for Black communities worldwide.

Black women had positive and important roles in these structured organisations, even though their voices were generally overshadowed by men. One such woman was Stella Thomas, a founder-member of the League of Coloured Peoples, despite the tendency of organisation recognition and representation being attributed predominantly to Harold Moody. Stella Thomas, was the first West African woman to be called to the bar in 1933, and later, became the first Nigerian female magistrate in 1942. Another feminist-social-activist member of the PAC in the United Kingdom, was Una Marson. A poet, playwright and columnist; Marson, would undertake a pivotal role as a programme content creator for the BBC radio Empire Services, during the WWII period. (Bourne, 2018: 71–2) She was educated in the cultural, political, and social lives in Jamaica and assumed the post of the organisation's secretary. At the fifth Pan-African Congress in 1945, Amy Jacques Garvey, journalist, publisher, an avid activist and the second wife of Marcus Garvey; who spoke out about the marginalisation of black women, even during the conference. Minimal mention of issues pertinent to women was raised, causing her to intervene, exclaiming it would seem that women had been, "shunted into the social background, to be child bearer" (Bryan, Dadzie, and Scafe 1985: 135).

Last but nowhere least, a spotlight will be shone on force of nature Claudia Jones, who played a powerful role in the black struggle in Britain. A brief summary of her achievements relating to Caribbeans' struggles for fair treatment, acceptance, and self-improvement is drawn upon later in this chapter.

For Caribbeans' living in Britain, it became all too clear that they needed to stand up for their rights. In light of this tragedy, Kelso Cochrane's funeral became part of a protest rally. Caribbeans felt compelled to collectively come together to protect their welfare and well-being, and that of their fellow Caribbean brethren wherever possible, especially those who were more vulnerable to being attacked:

> To begin with there were very few black women around. They didn't really come onto the scene until the mid-fifties. That was when the real hostilities began. With our arrival, they found a place where they could focus all their psychological hatred. They knew if they attacked a Black woman on the street with her kids, she wasn't in a position to fight back. (Bryan, Dadzie, and Scafe 1985: 133, 134)

The Notting Hill riots attracted worldwide attention to the racist backlash vented towards the Caribbean neighbourhood residents. It was condemned by Caribbean governments, who forwarded an official complaint to the British government. Official government reports revealed the unwillingness of local factories to recruit black workers. The issue of mixed-race relationships, especially between black men and white women in relationships, was another factor escalating the tensions.

Figure 6: Norman Manley visits Notting Hill, 1958.

Norman Manley, Chief Minister of Jamaica, 6th September 1958. Having a friendly conversation and shaking hands with a Caribbean Notting Hill resident after rioting in the area.

Source: Hulton Archive, Photo by Ron Burton / Stringer.

There were differing opinions stemming from media news publications, such as *The Times,* who printed, "the ugliest fighting". On the other hand, the *Daily Mail* sought readers' viewpoints as to whether the white mass population should see fit for immigration to the United Kingdom to continue: "Should we let them carry on coming in?" This would result in the political and public opinions to diverge.

In contrast, the Caribbean community was appalled, dismayed, and upset by what was construed as the police's outright suppression of the racial bias which fuelled the riots in the first place. In the wake of the aftermath of the Notting Hill riots, more than four thousand black people returned home to the Caribbean. The repercussions from the riots of 1958 in Nottingham and Notting Hill also resulted in a series of political debates about setting limitations to immigration in Britain's inner cities as well as conversations on how best to address the problem of racism and ensuing racial tensions.

The mandate would be to (a) control the number of immigrants entering Britain, and (b) devise ways to combat racial discrimination. The introduction of the Commonwealth Immigrants Act 1962 saw a sharp rise of migration to Britain in 1961. Both Conservative and Labour politicians were aware that limiting the flow of immigration would not be received well by Commonwealth governments, but due to negative public opinions at the time, the National Front Party was created in 1967, adding to the prevailing chants, "Send them back home", and, "No more in this country", along with graffiti popping up saying, "Keep Britain White" which caused the government to be seen as appeasing the English masses (Bushnell and Warren 2010: 9).

Peter Griffiths, Conservative MP constituent for Smethwick, Birmingham, won the seat over former Labour constituent Patrick Gordon Walker by using the popular racist slogan, "If you want a nigger for a neighbour vote Labour" (Bushnell and Warren 2010: 10). This would prompt a visit by Malcolm X to the Birmingham-Smethwick district in 1965 to support and show solidarity with the black Caribbean community living there.

Enoch Powell, a Conservative MP in the shadow cabinet, would become renowned for his "rivers of blood" speech, which took place in Birmingham in April 1968. The speech helped to reinforce and stimulate public opinion and gave credibility to the racial argument in favour of needing to do more to effectively tackle the race problem. Powell argued that because, "*the* failure of successive governments to act decisively to halt immigration in the 1950s", had led to a situation where, "more drastic measures", were required to solve the problem. Powell's inflammatory speech led him to be sacked from the shadow cabinet. However, Powell did have a strong following primarily from the white working-class segment of the population. A march by London dock workers, shouting chants such as, "Bye, bye blackbird", gained huge momentum, along with a petition containing more than thirty thousand signatures calling for Powell's position to be reinstated (Bushnell and Warren 2010: 11; Solomos 1989: 67, 68).

[2]‘**Britain For the British**’.

Figure 7: Petition to end All Immigration into Britain

Source: Hulton Archive, Photo by Keystone/Stringer.

The 1962 Immigrants Act would be followed up with the Commonwealth Immigrants Act 1968. It added the element of needing to have a parent or grandparent born in Britain in addition to the compulsory employment voucher. Then came the Immigration Act 1971, that rescinded employment vouchers in favour of twelve-month work permits, ensuring short-term stays only. And with this, primary immigration from the Caribbean and Asia practically came to a halt. Primary immigration means that no single person can migrate to Britain. If a settled immigrant residing in Britain later sent for family members to join him or her, the new immigrants were to be classified as secondary immigrants. The 1971 act gave way to an upgrade in 1973, and then came the Nationality Act of 1981. The latter basically made British and Commonwealth citizenship separate categories, cancelling any possibility of a British Commonwealth–born citizen to any consideration whatsoever or any type of inherent claim or access to British citizenship. This sealed the openings for successive Commonwealth immigration. Such was the aversion of the native British population (Bushnell and Warren 2010: 6, 8, 9; Murdoch 2012: 97, 98).

---

[2] A massive march took place on 25th August 1972, led by the Smithfield meat porters headed toward the Home Office, in receipt of a petition which called for an end to all immigration into Britain.

The Notting Hill, or North Kensington riots were sparked by black and white working-class families living in substandard slum conditions. Many were controlled by rogue slum landlords, such as Peter Rachman, inspired by the 1957 Rent Act (Phillips and Phillips 1999: 190; Fryer 1984: 378; Lowe 2011: 94; Lund 2011: 57) which courted the exploitation of the poorest members of society. This included the practice of seizing opportunities to evict long-standing white residents living in poor housing conditions to accommodate new immigrant arrivals at higher rental prices.

The ensuing tensions caused blacks to become scapegoats for all the feelings of frustration and lack of fit for purpose properties. This led to violence directed towards blacks living in the vicinity by fascist white youths (Fryer 1984: 378, 379; Mullard 1973: 48).

Owing to an escalating unwillingness by the host agencies to support Caribbeans trying to improve their settlement conditions and racial discrimination permeating every aspect of daily life (Fryer 1984: 385), one progress route was to create self-help and self-empowerment strategies by banding together in a community-spirited way to help ease the burdens and to become more politically organised. They founded the organisation for the Protection of Coloured Peoples, whereby Caribbean residents in Notting Hill embarked on a rent strike until housing repairs were attended to (Bushnell and Warren 2010: 8). Caribbeans looked for ways to normalise their situations and relieve their burdens by consolidating their efforts; networking and conversing with one another, as well as by supporting each other to acquire stable accommodation and to thrive.

Establishing black hairdressing parlours was one way. It was an occupation taken up by Interviewee 8 (see chapter 4), who set up a hairdressing business in her home. In any case, even if Caribbean women weren't barred entry to white English/ European establishments, it's unlikely, especially at the time, those hairdressers would be acquainted with the methods specific to the needs of black women when it came to styling Afro-Caribbean hair. Black hairdressing parlours would become a necessary space for Caribbean women to socialise, vent, and bond with each other, united in their common daily struggles as aptly conveyed: "Going along to have your hair pressed or relaxed was a social event, an opportunity to meet and exchange stories with other women … the hairdresser was well-placed to give advice, support and reassurance to others" (Bryan, Dadzie, and Scafe 1985, 131).

Caribbean hairdressers were well positioned to facilitate the organisation of the "pardner" scheme, where Caribbean men and women pooled their resources (Selvon 1990: 20), banking money collectively into savings schemes. Each month or week one "saver" collected a lump sum pay-out over a set period, until everyone received their shares. Then the scheme restarted.

This scheme is commonly known as pardner by Jamaicans or *sou-sou* by Trinidadians, derived from the African name *susu*. The Chinese also use pardners, which are called *hui* or *wee chen* (Voice-online 2014). Pardners are rotating savings and credit associations (ROSCA). Credit unions grew with the use of registered pardner services, such as the registered community UK-based pardner company business set up by a Jamaican-born woman, Portia Grant (Voice-online 2014). Pardners were frequently the only practical solution for Caribbeans aspiring to home ownership.

The use of pardners resonates with the spoken experiences of the case-study women. The majority were involved in pardner schemes. Interviewee 7 still follows the pardner tradition, and as the so-called banker, she continues to be responsible for organising pardners which involves holding and issuing the pay-out of collective savings.

> It was mainly women who set up the pardners; nine out of ten of the pardna schemes had a woman in charge of them. It was done on a village or family basis. Whoever's needs were greater, they got the deposit on a house. It was the women who held on to the money and paid down the deposit, but still no home could be put in her name. Later people started to have selling parties. It helped to pay the mortgage, but it also provided us with somewhere to go. That's why they started. (Bryan, Dadzie, and Scafe 1985: 131)

The above quote mirrors the experience of Interviewee 7, who bought a property with her husband. Her name was not on the deed, despite investing the larger sum into the property:

> We paid three and a half thousand pounds for the house (in 1958) … This house had two kitchens, two bathrooms, and a shower … there was only four houses on the whole street like ours … when we bought the house my name was not on the freehold, because in those days women had no rights, so the man had all the power.

Seven out of the eight case-study women spoke about their involvement with pardner schemes. Interviewee 7 said, "I started to run 'pardners' as this enabled us Caribbeans to help each other to buy our own houses; most times this was the only way we could get properties to buy." And in the words of Interviewee 8, "I was in a pardner … still am to the present day … We couldn't do nothing without a pardner." (See chapter 4.)

The pardner originated in Africa and was brought to Jamaica by African slaves, who used it in the beginning as a way to purchase their freedom. The pardner came to represent a mechanism for liberation (Voice-online 2014).

Established Caribbean proprietors would go on to rent to fellow kinsmen (Sivanandan 1982: 6; hackney.gov.uk 2013).

Patterson explains that through resourcefulness, Caribbean folk started investing in run-down, short-lease houses, gradually extending to lengthier leaseholds until finally going on to obtain the freehold. In some cases, these houses were purchased with white sitting tenants (Patterson 1965: 161).

Another self-help occupation that black women embarked on as the numbers of women and children increased was child-minding services. This was due to the scarcity of nursery place admittance of Caribbean preschool children.

In terms of racism in education, it was pointed out by Carter (1987: 83–85) that in the borough of Haringey, in North London, Caribbeans became champions for resistance commencing from the late sixties, as documented in a *Race Today* pamphlet bringing issues to light. It stated that it was the beginning of a "Black Explosion", which would come to overshadow Haringey's white progressive movement. At the time, people lobbied for changes and improvements in education. It was the black struggle that would inform and challenge the status quo to revise the educational system over the following two decades. Post-war migration from the Caribbean intersected with a period of extensive trial runs in education in Britain. According to Carter, "Secondary, further and higher education was being expanded and the development of a Comprehensive system of Secondary education being debated and planned" (Carter 1987: 83).

The education system was being overhauled. This, in turn, caused instability, with teachers vacating positions at a rapid rate, creating a high turnover of teaching staff (see chapter 5, *Education*). Stemming from the post-WWII recovery years, accompanied with mass post-war immigration didn't mix well. Carter expressed that he, like many Caribbean parents, were initially conflicted when their children came home and spoke of their first encounters of racist taunts in school from teachers telling black children to "Go back home to the jungle." In Southall, London borough of Southwark, white parents went on the offensive about there being large numbers of Asian children in *their* schools. They were the first recipients of rising racially derived complaints. This resulted in The Department of Education and Science (DES), authorising a policy of dispersal. The publication of the DES circular (1965) '*The education of immigrants,*' would seek to appease concerned white parents, as well as easing the burden for overwhelmed teachers. It read:

> As the proportion of immigrant children in a school or class increases, the problems will become more difficult to solve, and the chances of assimilation more remote ... up to a fifth of immigrant children in any one group fit with reasonable ease, but if the proportion goes over about one-third in the school as a whole or in any one class, serious strains arise. (Carter 1987: 85)

This boiled down to the children of Caribbean migrants being perceived by the white host as uneducable and in larger numbers liable to affect the overall school educational performance. The 1965 DES circular led to several local authorities introducing a policy of dispersal, controlling the number of black pupils that would be allowed entry to any one school. The introduction of these protocols effectively rallied appalled Caribbean parents—as in the case of the borough of Haringey, North London, during the late sixties—to form an alliance between black teachers, parents, and community workers. It included a sprinkling of white liberal and anti-racist support. The alliance was to be known as the North London West Indian Association (NLWIA), founded in 1969, who fought back against the proposal in Haringey to "bus black children around the borough to avoid the development of 'ghetto' schools ... which would have far reaching educational repercussions" (Carter 1987: 87).

The NLWIA defended their case and won. At this time, the NLWIA was already linked to the West Indian Standing Conference, which was born out of the 1958 race riots. As a result of the overwhelming failings targeted at immigrant children, the black community in Haringey would later begin setting up their own supplementary schools (Carter 1987: 90–92).

Church attendance was amongst the issues expressed during the women's case studies. As documented in Sivanandan (1982: 6; also, Phillips and Phillips 1999:149), Caribbeans were often rejected from the church, apparently in particular Anglican churches, and excused by the vicars as black visitors to the church caused the white congregation to withdraw their attendance. This encouraged Caribbeans to set up their own churches and social clubs to combat the situation.

Another Caribbean cultural form borne of self-empowerment, solidarity, as well as positive and popular expression, and in response to the racially motivated murder of Kelso Cochrane (1959) and the riots in Notting Hill (1958) was marked by the commencement of London's Notting Hill Carnival.

The brainchild of Claudia Jones, a Trinidadian political activist, this event first commenced at St Pancras Town Hall in 1959, and extended to the streets of Notting Hill from 1965. It grew to become an integral part of British society. (hackney.gov. uk 2013; Murdoch 2012: 103, 104).

Claudia Jones was born in Trinidad on 21 February 1915. At the time, Trinidad was still a British colonial territory. She and her family migrated to Harlem, New York, at the impressionable age of eight. There she was exposed to the suffering and harsh displays of American racism. Coming from humble roots, she learnt only too well the daily struggles of black women on the lower rung of the socio-economic ladder. Women who were more susceptible to unemployment and forced into domestic and factory work to get by. It was these painful memories that inspired her to go into politics.

Claudia began working as an editor for publications by the Young Communist League. She grew evermore dedicated to engaging in anti-racist work. She became involved with the high-profile Scottsboro case, for which she vigorously campaigned, shining a light on discrepancies, gathering support, and raising awareness. Nine black men had been accused of raping two white women and were facing the death penalty. The Scottsboro case would go on for four years.

Her endless campaigning for their release resulted in a re-trial, where five of the men were exonerated. The remaining four received life sentences despite the fact that one of the female accusers withdrew her original testimony. This case put Claudia on the political radar, and she was seen as an agitator against racism. And led her to come under scrutiny and later attack, especially during the Joseph McCarthy witch-hunts in 1951, which led to her being charged with offences against the United States. She was arrested and sent to prison for one year, even amid the international outcry and campaigning against the allegations directed at her. Following her release, she was deported (Bryan, Dadzie, and Scafe 1985: 136; Davis 1982: 167, 171).

This led Claudia to travel to Britain in 1956. She came to the United Kingdom with a heightened awareness of the mechanisms of racism. Although more covertly veiled on occasions, it was no less impacting for the black recipient amid its inflicting woes and wreaking havoc on Caribbean people's senses of self-worth and dignity. Her work against racism continued, and she became engrossed with the struggle of Caribbeans. She worked with grassroots organisations and campaigns to tackle British racism in every area and at every level of the socio-economic structure informing everyday living necessary to survival and self-improvement, including housing, jobs, and education.

She collaborated with Amy Jacques Garvey and started the *West Indian Gazette* (*WIG*) in 1958. This, the first campaigning black newspaper, gained much positive attraction and support from famous advocates for black progress and social change. They included Paul Robeson, amongst others (Bryan, Dadzie, and Scafe 1985: 136–139).

Figure 8: Claudia Jones at the WIG

Claudia at the offices of the West Indian Gazette (WIG) situated at 250 Brixton Road, South London, 1962. Jones founded the newspaper in 1958 and remained its editor until her death.

Source: Archive Photos, FGP / Staff via Getty Images

Claudia sent a clear message as an anti-imperialist. At the beginning of the civil rights movement in 1964, she wrote in the *Black American Journal* article "Freedomways",

> The citizens of the "Mother of Democracy" do not yet recognise that the roots of racialism in Britain were laid in the eighteenth and nineteenth centuries through British conquests in India, Africa and great parts of Asia, as well as the British Caribbean. All the resources of official propaganda and education, the super-structure of British imperialism, were permeated with projecting the oppressed colonial peoples as lesser breeds, as "inferior-coloured peoples" "savages" and the like—in short, "the white man's burden". (Rodney, 2018: 245) These rationalisations all served to build a justification for wholesale exploitation, extermination and looting of the islands by British imperialism. The great wealth of present-day British monopoly capital was built on the robbery of coloured peoples by such firms as Unilever and the East Africa Company to Tate & Lyle and Booker Bros. In the Caribbean. (Bryan, Dadzie, and Scafe 1985: 137; Rodney, 2018: 161, 175, 239, 253)

Notably, Interviewee 1 held a similar perception and would set perpetrators straight when faced with their racist and ignorant remarks by letting them know that "England was called the Mother Country; so, this is why when people would tell me to go back home, I would say that I have a right to be here as the wealth in my country was squeezed out from Britain … they drained all of our natural resources such as the Bauxite … The English people who made such remarks knew nothing about Geography or History and I was amazed that people were so uneducated" (see chapter 4).

There is so much more to be said the incredible legacy of Claudia Jones and her contribution to what would become one of the foundations for the formation of the Black Power movement. But for the purpose of this discourse, her story has to be curtailed. Claudia's work would extend across the globe, to Japan, China, and Russia.

In Britain, she was part of the hunger strikes situated outside the South African embassy, campaigning to free Nelson Mandela (1963). She was a representative for black people and humanitarian causes worldwide.

Tragically, soon after returning to Britain from China, on Christmas Day 1964, she died in her sleep having suffered a stroke.

Paul Robeson paid tribute at her funeral: "Claudia Jones continued in her day the heroic tradition of Harriet Tubman, of Sojourner Truth—the struggle for negro liberation and women's rights, for human dignity and fulfilment" (Bryan, Dadzie, and Scafe 1985: 139).

Figure 8.1: The First ever Notting Hill Carnival, 1959.

30th January 1959, was the date that the first ever carnival took place as an indoor event, organised by Claudia Jones. It was created in response to the racial riots of the year prior, in August 1958. It was referred to as the Caribbean carnival or the West Indian Gazette Carnival, and took place at St. Pancras Town Hall. The photo image shows a couple dancing at the event.

Source: Mirrorpix via Getty Images; Photo by Daily Mirror.

Figure 9: Caribbean Migrant Protest, 1959

Caribbean migrants can be seen peacefully protesting against racial discrimination. Riots broke out in August 1958 in Notting Hill, following attacks from groups of white youths (Bushnell and Warren 2010: 7). The protest took place two weeks after the murder of Kelso Cochrane, 1st June 1959. The protestor to the far right is holding a placard with Kelso's name and portrait.

Source: Hulton Archive, Photo by John Franks / Stringer

Figure 10: Notting Hill Neighbourhood Residents, 1954

These two young men where commonly referred to as spivs, or petty criminals who were known for their dealings in illegal black-market goods, during the period following WWII, where there were many shortages due to rationing.

Source: Picture Post / Stringer / Getty Images

Figure 11: Teddy-Boys Awaiting Trial 1958

The photo was taken on, 4th September 1958, a short time after the four men's court appearance at Tower Bridge Police Court, London, for their involvement in the Notting Hill race riots. From left to right, John Lewis, Ronald Cooper, Alfred Harper and Peter Thomas.

Source: Hulton Getty Archive, Photo by Ron Case / Stringer

CHAPTER 3

Research Methodology

This chapter looks at the methodologies used to research the housing experiences and aspirations of Caribbean migration *Windrush*-era women. A mainly qualitative approach was adopted (Creswell 2014: 215–230).

The research subjects were sorted by engaging with family, friends, and connected associations or kinship ties within the community, as well as extended familial sources in extended London regions. The women's case studies document primary information relating to a generation that is now elderly and ever diminishing in number. This situation is amplified because women were a marginal group at the time of the *Windrush*-generation migration. Therefore, seeking to preserve such an invaluable cultural legacy was a necessary goal. Realistically, obtaining highly sensitive information of this nature meant the samples could only be coaxed from subjects with some degree of personable association. It was necessary to establish a level of trust and earned respect by being known to and meeting the informants' approval to facilitate engagement.

Initial informal exchanges were arranged in person or by phone to explain the purpose of the case-study research. This allowed interviewees to make informed decisions as to whether they were happy to proceed. The potential subject was not compelled to decide there and then.

Once agreeable to participating, arrangements commenced to meet with each candidate at dates and times of their choosing and where they felt comfortable to conduct the interview. On occasions, unforeseen circumstances would crop up, causing meeting dates to be rescheduled. Interviews were conducted at the informants' home. Only in one case did the informant prefer to meet in a neutral setting, which was my mother's home. The interview was carried out in a private room to maintain confidentiality and avoid unnecessary distractions.

Before commencing with each interview, the case-study consent form was read. It outlined ethical considerations to be followed, such as maintaining confidentiality, and explained the research process and tools used, such as voice recorders. After the informants or interviewees were asked if they had any questions and if they were happy to proceed, they were then asked to sign the consent form. I countersigned each form.

On average, the interviews all required travelling considerable distances to meet with the informants; this had to be factored into the overall time consumed in completing each interview. Therefore, each interview took five to seven hours.

Another challenging factor presenting itself was that sometimes, the informant became temporarily unable to remember some of their housing dates or addresses. To help individuals remember, they would be encouraged to recall memorable events in their lives, such as the births of children, marriages, travel, or changes of employment. With a prolonged memory block, we sometimes kept moving forward until, during the course of recalling events about later housing history, earlier housing information returned to mind.

Semi-structured interviews have been conducted with women to help prompt them a little. This was a useful method in alleviating awkwardness in knowing where to start. The aim was to facilitate the natural flow of the informants' recollections as much as possible. There was only enough steering of their thought processes to maintain the flow of recounting housing details from newly arrived female Caribbean migrants in the United Kingdom to present-day British naturalised home occupants (Biggam 2011: 127–129).

The women's personal housing experiences, tenure changes, patterns, and recurring themes were mapped over a considerable historical time frame by way of case-study comparison (Biggam 2011: 126, 127, 129; Swetnam and Swetnam 2000: 128).

The information was collated by the use of a systemised format for each woman described as an interviewee (see chapter 4).

Each interviewee's chart has been numbered to recognise each interviewee without compromising anonymity. For added effectiveness, colour charts were used as an easy identifier for each interviewee to prevent the possibility of mistakenly adding information to the wrong chart.

Professional conduct and gaining trust were paramount in actively engaging with the interviewee. It was necessary to connect her feelings and sensitivities and to respect the interviewees' decisions about disclosures. For instance, in the throes of an interview, the interviewee may divulge information that she would later want to keep private and undocumented. The interviewee's wishes were always respected.

CHAPTER 4

Caribbean Migration: The Windrush Women's Case Studies

This chapter presents a summary of the interviews conducted with the Caribbean *Windrush* women. Eight women form the primary research focus of the case studies, which are highlighted in colour-coded charts as follows:

Colour Identifier Interview Chart

✓ *Interviewee 1*
✓ *Interviewee 2*
✓ *Interviewee 3*
✓ *Interviewee 4*
✓ *Interviewee 5*
✓ *Interviewee 6*
✓ *Interviewee 7*
✓ *Interviewee 8*

The intent of qualitative research is to understand a particular social situation, event, role, group, or interaction. It is largely an investigative process where the researcher gradually makes sense of a social phenomenon by contrasting, replicating, cataloguing and classifying the object of study. The researcher enters the informants' world and through ongoing interaction, sees the informants' perspectives and meanings. (Creswell 2014: 205)

Caribbean Women's Migration: *Windrush* Housing Experiences and Aspirations

Housing History since Arrival in the UK, Interviewee 1, from 1955 to 10.01.2014

Location/Tenure Type	Year/ Duration	Experiences: Main Events Happening at the Time	Employment—Job Title/Role	Social Networks, Family, Friends, School, Work, Church
14 Westbank, N16 Private landlord (Jewish). Rental; shared accommodation. Attic room.	1955–1956	I left Jamaica on 15 April. I travelled by ship, the *Castell Verde*, an Italian ship. My fare cost £75, which my sister sent to me. I remember because when I was counting out the money, I was amazed as I had never seen so much money. It took seventeen days to travel, and it was a wonderful experience. I landed on May 1. From Jamaica, we docked at Italy then took a chartered train, reserved for Caribbean immigrants, through the continent to Spain, then Switzerland, over to France, and then a ferry over to Dover. From Dover I boarded the train to Victoria. I didn't even think of the weather! And I didn't have much warm garments. My sister came to meet me with a maxi-length royal-blue coat and matching hat. I couldn't get my luggage that day. We travelled on the underground from Victoria to Manor House; it was an experience going up and down the escalator. We took the 253 bus, as it still is now, fifty-eight years ago.	Worked in the rag trade in a dress factory as machinist and filled in any extra jobs that needed doing. Earned £3, 10s per week High Road, corner of Crowland Road, N15	I had just turned eighteen years old. I was living with my sister in shared accommodation with other tenants. We talked for most of the night, and then amazingly, my sister woke me at 7 a.m. and told me to get ready for work! After seventeen days at sea, I was extremely tired, but my sister said that nobody rests in London. In Jamaica I worked for 18 shillings but with no expenses, so having to do everything out of my wages was quite daunting.
Wray Crescent, Hornsey N8 Terraced house with basement, private. Landlady (Jamaican) rental; shared accommodation.	1956–1957	After falling out with my sister, the accommodation situation became very tedious and unsettled. I found myself moving from place to place for very short periods. It got so bad at one stage that I was sharing a room with someone that I didn't know and even forced to share the same bed with them until eventually I got to know the woman. We ended up becoming good friends.	Simpsons Tailoring, doing basting, earning £4 per week. In Stoke Newington High St. E8	I felt cut off from my family and quite isolated. The few black people around weren't enough to supply the influx. The English wouldn't take us in. "No Blacks, No Irish, No Dogs." So you wouldn't even knock on their door to perplex them. The Jewish were real businesspeople and made a whole lot of money off us, but we had no choice.

| Other tenement properties; unable to remember all. | 1956–1957 | I found it so hard to make ends meet, so I left the rag trade and went into engineering. | Went to work in an engineering factory in Northumberland Park, earning £4, 50s per week. | Every Christmas the company used to treat its workers by taking them to the theatre, such as the Palladium, and ice-skating shows. We went to France, Calais, Boulogne, and Dunkirk. They used to put on nice dances which gave its workers the chance to get dressed up. The workers paid subs in order to pay for these treats as otherwise there would be no opportunity to experience these grandiose events as workers such as myself could not afford it. What was so nice is that everyone mixed, from the directors to the cleaners. And when we lowly workers put ourselves together, we would cause a stir and bring colour and vibrancy! They admired us Caribbeans for that; everyone complimented us … it was uplifting for English people, especially coming out of the War. You worked hard, but everyone clubbed together. |

Broadwater Road N17 Private rental accommodation; landlord. West Indian, Jamaican, Shared accommodation.	End of 1957	I met the man who was to become my husband. His life was as unsettled as mine at the time, but we got together and started dating within a couple of months of meeting one another. In the end, because of our limited earnings and wanting to be more stable, we ended up deciding to live together in order to pool resources and ease the strain. None of us was accustomed to this sort of life, coming from a stable home life in Jamaica and living with our parents ... We just kind of fell into it ... We weren't happy about it, so we did not tell anyone about our living together as that would be frowned upon, and we would have been disgraced.	Only the rich had a television of about nine to twelve inches, and BBC1 was the only station. Everyone in the Caribbean community aimed to buy a blue spot music centre with radio. Most of us didn't like the pub culture and started to make our own house parties ... English people didn't like this and sometimes used to call us noisy. We also used to go to the pictures a lot ... it was warm and cosy in there. People would use paraffin heaters; some used to have coal fires, but that was for the weekend. You were never lovely and warm ... One night I slept in my overcoat ... There was no hot running water. In the bath there was a meter, and you had to put in 2p ... Things were very cheap, but wages were also cheap. £1, 1shilling was called a Ginny.
Westbank (Temporary in order to plan the wedding.)		It was love at first sight. We met in October 1957, and we started saving and planning together from the outset. So by June 1958, we were married. Within that duration we put together £500, and this allowed us to have a beautiful wedding. We had our wedding reception in the attic of the rented room at Westbank, at my sister's. the announcement of our wedding gave my sister and me the opportunity to rekindle our relationship and make up. Being in the rag trade, my sister and I made all the bridesmaids' dresses, and my friend was a Milner, so she made the hats!	Being from the Caribbean, we were part of the Commonwealth, so I was used to the currency. England was called the mother country; so this is why when people would tell me to go back home, I would say that I have a right to be here as the wealth in my country was squeezed out from Britain; they drained all of our resources such as the bauxite. The English people who made such remarks knew nothing about geography or history, and I was amazed that people were so uneducated.

Property	Dates		
29 Willoughby Lane, N17 House converted into flats. Third-floor flat. Private rental.	1959–1962	This accommodation was a big step up as it was our first flat that we had a whole floor to ourselves, not sharing with others. We were able to buy our furniture on hire purchase with my sister standing in as guarantee for the first time. We went to Star Furniture in Finsbury Park, and this was one of the biggest events in my life.	My husband strived to get a profession, so he started attending evening classes at Tottenham Technical College, training to be a welder.
Colsterworth Road N15 Flat conversion; part furnished and was able to rent out one room to my friend to help out with the costs. Rent was approximately £4–4.5 per week. Private rental.	1962–1965	A friend shared the living room, kitchen, and toilet. There was no bathroom in those days. You went to the public baths across the street. We took the master bedroom and a small bedroom. My friend had a good-size double room. The living room was a single room but cosy, enough for an armchair at least. It served as a communal area.	When my sister-in-law came from Jamaica to do her nursing training, she stayed with us and used that room and slept on the bed settee.
		With a savings of £500 to £600, you could get on to the property ladder, even if you started off with a leasehold and eventually bought the freehold. The war finished in 1945 or 1946, and white people didn't want to invest in property as they went through a lot with the bombing of their properties. Flats came up, and it was the new thing … When we started investing in property, they thought we were mad! But you had to be bold to gain. There was no central heating, and most houses' toilets were outside. In those days, there was public baths all over; you were lucky if you got a bath once a week. The English would wash in the kitchen sink. We bought a basin to wash ourselves and basin to wash the dishes in.	When we would share accommodation, we would befriend each other as there were not as many of us living here and save together. Using pardner schemes became a useful way to help us to accumulate money to get our own properties. This is a commitment we would make to help ourselves, and we would also use credit unions and pay into this.
93 Mountview Road, Finsbury Park, N4 Double-front, semi-detached house. Mortgaged property.	1965–1969	My husband and I shared this property with my eldest sister. This was a beautiful and spacious house. My first and second children were born in this property.	When my sister made the decision to immigrate to the USA, we were unable to afford to stay; my sister said once the property was sold, we could send her share of the proceeds.

Property	Dates	Notes	Occupation	Faith / Church
Sydney Avenue, Palmers Green, N13 2-bedroom flat.	1969–1970	My third child was born, and we needed more space.		
82 Craven Park Road, South Tottenham, N15 3-bedroom terraced house. Mortgaged property.	1970–1982	I did not like this house. I felt that it was small so ended up putting on two extensions. There was a strong Caribbean community on this road and within the surrounding area.	An orderly, Prince of Wales Hospital, N17. 1970–1979	I started to attend St Bartholomew's C of E Anglican Church, Craven Park Rd N15 and became an active member of the congregation.
Radley Road, Tottenham N17. 5-bedroom semi-detached house. Bought outright.	1982–Present	Considerable improvements have been made to this property; an extension has given me a spacious kitchen diner, which had been an aspiration after many years of having a very small kitchen. I've gone from a 4-to 5-bedroom property and put in a wet room. Between the 08-01-2001, until 21-01-2002, my mother embarked on a series of *Windrush* migration oral history interviews with interviewer Polly Russell, conducted at her sister's home in Leicester. These oral recordings are held in the British Library under the category "Food (Oral-history/Food): Green, Bernice (1 of 25) Food: From Source to Salespoint." Mum's story is centred around Caribbean cuisine and catering, but she also spoke in depth about her early upbringing and family life growing up in Jamaica. Mum goes on to speak about her experiences of family as well as the Caribbean neighbourhood community, which we grew up amongst; the church and the many experiences that shaped her life, living in the UK. This beautiful legacy left by her for the benefit of family and for future generations of Caribbeans living in the UK to remember the history and contributions of the black people that came before them. Adding to the rich Caribbean footprint made, and to impact positively on everyday working-class people living in Britain's multiracial society.	Teaching assistant, Home Economic Department, Skinners Girls Upper School, Stamford Hill N16. Worked until retirement in 1996.	As my faith and self-confidence grew, I began to do the intercessions at church and cook Caribbean cuisine for the church fairs and various events which went down very well.

Caribbean Women's Migration: *Windrush* Housing Experiences and Aspirations

Housing History since Arrival in the UK, Interviewee 2, from 1961 to 08.02.2014				
Location/ Tenure Type	Year/ Duration	Experiences: Main Events Happening at the Time	Employment—Job Title/Role	Social Networks, Family, Friends, School, Work, Church
Chiswick High Road, W4 Terraced house, private rental, shared accommodation.	November 1961–1962	I travelled by ship, the SS *Begonia*. I came in November; it was freezing cold. My dad wanted me to have a better life; my elder sisters were already here and nieces and nephews. At school in Jamaica, I was taught that England was the motherland, and the streets were paved with gold; but it was a shock! I never realised that there were so many poor people, and I found their lifestyles strange and different. Bread used to be lying on the pavement, and they used newspaper to wrap the bread. Then a dog would come along and take the bread ... Fish and chips were also wrapped in newspaper. In Jamaica, newspaper was seen as unhealthy and wouldn't be used to wrap food in. Bathing in the kitchen sink was also another custom that was new to Caribbeans. In those days, it was so cold we used to set the jelly out on the windowsill. We would put our butter, meat, and milk on the windowsill to preserve it. There were a lot of public baths.	Smith's Crisps factory on Great Western Road. This was my first experience of work. We worked on a conveyor belt. Once I got into the rhythm, it was all right. We, the black ones, had to work harder than the white ones. When you complained, it would be like going against the rules of the company.	My father never came to England, although he helped his children to come. My mother died when I was five years old. My father was a port worker. When my mother died, he was left with five children to care for. On arriving in London, I was living with my sister, and I was unhappy because being older than I, she had a tendency to treat me like a child. I had to do everything in the house before I could go out and look for work ... I also had to look after my niece and nephews, which included taking them to school. My niece and I had one room with the cooker in the passage and the paraffin heater. The washing line was over the bed. My niece and I had to share the same bed. A lot of people went back home because they couldn't take it ... I sent for my husband and children gradually. I have five children; only one was born here.

Park Road, Hornsey N8 Terraced house, private rental; shared accommodation.	May 1962–October 1962	I stopped with members of the family for a short while.	Still working at Smith's Crisps.	You moved around a lot in those days … The only white people who would rent to us were Jewish people. White guys would ask us the time. … At 12 noon, your shadow sets under your feet. They would call us monkeys.
Winchelsea Road, N17 Terraced House, Jamaican landlord. Private rental, shared accommodation.	Late 1962—1963		MK Electricals.	When you met with other black people, they would be friendly and socialise. We didn't go to pubs, but black people would hold their own house parties. Whoever came home first would cook; we were a family. We would band together; even at work black elders would take on a mothering role and care about your welfare as a younger black person.
Clinton Road, N15 Three-storey terraced house. Jamaican landlord, but he did not live in the property.	1963–1964	Downstairs there was a family from Barbados; upstairs there were two sisters sharing a room; on the middle floor was a woman from Jamaica. I was on the top floor. After I had my last child, I needed a more suitable place.	Leibertute, a factory that specialises in children's paints, pencils, crayons, and paint books. This was also conveyor-belt work. A lot of people from the Caribbean, both men and women, worked there. We had charge-hands who would pick on people they took a dislike to. They would find any excuse to pick on the black workers, so this was hard. White people felt that they were superior to you as a black person.	

Property	Dates	Housing notes	Work	Notes
Mount Pleasant Road, N17 Terraced house. Jamaican landlord.	1964, for a short while.	I had my own kitchen. The landlord promised table and chairs, but he didn't honour this arrangement. I washed up and started cooking, then I popped to the shops. And when I returned, I turned on the tap, but the water wouldn't go down. It turned out the landlord tampered with the pipe under the sink and then accused me of damaging the pipe. He insisted that I move out.		Sometimes the Jamaican landlords tried to take advantage of young women.
St Loy's Road, N17 Terraced house, Jamaican landlord	1964–1966		Thornes Electrical, Brimsdowne, EN3 I taught new workers how to make mobilisers and burglar alarms.	
Glenwood Road, N15 2-bedroom flat.	1966–1967	I was able to send for two of my children, but the property was not large enough to accommodate the rest of my children.	Tape Recorder Wingate Estate, High Road N17 I used to make tape recorders; we had to twist and solder the wire. You move on to assembling the parts, and then you go on to complete the whole tape recorder on the mother board and you have to test it.	
Glaserton Road, N16 3-bedroom flat.	1967–1969	Partially furnished property. My other two children came over from Jamaica. I had the upstairs flat, that consisted of the first and second floors. There was a sitting tenant downstairs.	Scholl's Shoe Factory	After working at Scholl's, I thought that I did not want to work in anymore factories.

| Elm Park Avenue, South Tottenham, N15 / 3-bedroom terraced house. Bought outright. | 1969–present | I was asked by Mr Norman to train his nephew. I became ill and was off work for two weeks. When I returned to work, Mr Norman told me that he was so sorry, but the company was going into liquidation and, therefore, my post would have to be terminated with immediate effect. I was very sorry as I was happy working for Norman Stanley. I decided to go to the job centre straightaway to look for a new job. When I arrived, I saw my post advertised, so I decided to apply. The job centre sent me to Norman Stanley, and I brought my English friend as a witness. When I arrived, Mr Norman was shocked to see me. I said, "Mr Norman, you said you were closing down, but you're not. It seems that after I have trained your nephew that you want to put him in my job." Although I knew that it was pointless to get my job back, as they would only find an excuse to sack me, I demanded my full pay. I went to Tottenham Advice Bureaux.

At that time there was no Employment Act to protect me from racism, so I could not sue. However, the Advice Bureaux demanded that Mr Norman pay me my months' notice, holiday pay, and sick pay, whereas before, I was denied all of this.

I have put a conservatory on to my house and remodelled the kitchen. I had an outside toilet which I brought inside and added a shower. | Norman Stanley Estate Agents: Doing accounts and collecting the rents for Abbey National Bank.

I left due to racism.

Accounting coordinator, Tiverton Estate, N15.

Howard Wall, assistant supervisor in accounts.

At Howard Wall, the supervisor was an Englishwoman, and she would say that when she went to the West End, she would see lots of black people doing shopping and buying the best things. She'd say, "Where do they get the money from." She would show resentment and amazement towards black people who bought their houses and drove nice cars … but I would say that the money that they would take to go on holiday all the time, we did not, but we would save. She would emphasize that she was not talking about me, but I knew different. So eventually, I left the job because I did not feel comfortable. | I did a lot of training 1984–87 in office practice, and I did a lot of temping jobs; this also enabled me to work around my children. I gained many skills, such as accounting. I learnt information technology and went on to teach this at Bounds Green College. I also did voluntary work at Tottenham Technical College. |

Caribbean Women's Migration: *Windrush* Housing Experiences and Aspirations

Housing History since Arrival in the UK, Interviewee 3, from 1962 to 18.01.2014

Location/Tenure Type	Year/Duration	Experiences: Main Events Happening at the Time	Employment— Job Title/Role	Social Networks, Family, Friends, School, Work, Church
Grove Park Rd off West Green Road A town house building or 3 storeys with basement. A huge house. Mortgaged property owned by my father, who was also the live-in landlord.	1962–1966	I came from a family of ten; three of us lived with my paternal grandmother. My mother and father were never married but lived very close to one another, so I saw my mother all the time; it could be likened to an extended family situation. At that time, the father's ruling took priority, so the decision was made by my father and paternal grandmother that I should come to England. I arrived in the height of the winter, there was the smog, and I got chill blades. We came by aeroplane into Gatwick Airport. It was a shock to the system; I was never prepared for what I came into. I arrived in thin cotton clothes, and psychologically, I was not prepared. There was no central heating in the house; my father rented out many of the rooms. But the nice thing was that the tenants became like family members.	Dad worked for British Rail; my stepmother worked in a factory.	My brother and I arrived together from Jamaica; I finished off my schooling in this country. I went to St Katherine C of E Secondary School before it merged with St David's to become St David's and St Katherine's. My head teacher's name was Ms Smith, and she was a woman who was small in stature but a powerful character, a force to be reckoned with, and who made a positive impact on me. I can't really say that I have had direct experiences of racism, although I have had instances where I have been aware of covert racism.
Hillside Road, N15 3-storey building rented from my cousin.	1966–1967	After ten years of living in the UK, my father and stepmother returned to Jamaica to live. I had an older brother already living in the UK; my brother became responsible for the payment of my rent as he was older than I. A gentleman from the same parish in Jamaica came to be renting a room with his wife; when he and his wife moved from Hillside Road to Mount Pleasant Road, they adopted me, so to speak, and we all moved to Mount Pleasant Road together.	I worked in the rag trade in Simpsons Tailors in the administration department. I earned approximately £7 per week.	I attended Tottenham Technical College learning doing Pittman shorthand in evening classes.

Mount Pleasant Road, N17 Large terraced house, private rental.	1967–1968	I had my first child in 1968.	Career-break.	
Kitchener Road, N17 Terraced house, private rental.	1968–1969	My "adoptive" parents bought this property. I had my second child and then got married in 1969.	Career-break, but worked temporarily at Mount Pleasant Post Office	
Dunlowe Avenue, N17 Terraced house, private rental.	1969–1973	I had my third child in 1971.		
Seymour Avenue, N17 Terraced house, mortgaged bought.	1973–2010	We bought the matrimonial home and lived there for 37 years, after which the marriage ended in divorce. I had 3 daughters with my husband. I started to become involved in throwing a pardner savings scheme. Gradually, my earning power increased with promotions in my job and so on; the pardner was useful in helping me maintain a better lifestyle for my family and also went towards family holidays.	I went back into full-time employment and began working for the London Borough of Camden, where I worked my way up to a managerial position. I continued to work for Camden until my retirement in 2007.	I started to become more involved in the church. My Mum passed away in early 2000, and then in November 2000, I got confirmed. This was a very poignant time and when my faith journey gained momentum. I have not looked back, and my faith has gone from strength to strength.
Chingford Road, E17 In Warner Flats, my home is self-contained with its own front door and shared garden. Mortgaged property.	2010–present	These flats are unique to Walthamstow, and they are very nice. Presently, I am living with my daughter. When I look at the situation holistically, I do not believe it is in my best interest to purchase property in the UK again. It makes more sense to reside between my daughters' homes.		I began to write the intercessions, and I am responsible for leading the Mother's Union in church. Also, as my faith grew, it has helped me to face personal challenges and confront them in a calm and dignified manner.
		In terms of future aspirations, I intend to purchase a property in Jamaica and commute between the UK and Jamaica as I have my children and grandchildren based here, who are an important part of my life, and I am not prepared to break that bond.		I love the Caribbean and still have an extensive family network there. There is also a strong returnee association in Jamaica, especially in the Kingston region, with their own gated community settings, where I can re-establish myself and keep my mind stimulated as it is important that I keep active.

Caribbean Women's Migration: *Windrush* Housing Experiences and Aspirations

Housing History since Arrival in the UK, Interviewee 4, from 1961 to 23.01.2014

Location/Tenure Type	Year/Duration	Experiences: Main Events Happening at the Time	Employment— Job Title/Role	Social networks, family, friends, School, Work, Church
Allerton Road, Stoke Newington, N16 Private rental, bedsit, shared facilities.	1961–1963	Jobs were hard to come by in Jamaica, and I had six children. I had been doing a little teaching. I had an aunt in England, so it was decided that it would be better for me to come over to England to try to make a better life. I left a lot of my clothes because people said you can't wear this, and you can't wear that, so I wondered, *what kind of place is this!* I arrived in the month of May, during the night. I had a bad experience with my travel… I came by plane, which cost about £75; and when I came out of the airport, I had to take a bus or train to Victoria; I can't remember now. I paid my fare, but I gave the ticket man too much money. I got a bit confused, and then I realised and went to dispute the matter, but the man who served me insisted he had given me the right change, so there was nothing I could do. Also, I missed my aunt, who came to meet me. In the end, someone else—a fellow countryman—came to meet me instead.	I got a job in a post office canteen in EC1, towards Holborn. I earned £5 per week.	I would send money back home to help to support my children that I had left in Jamaica.
Claybury Hospital, Essex, live-in accommodation.	Early 1963–mid-1963	The training was a good experience but a bit of a shock to the system as I never saw such things in Jamaica. My husband came over in mid-1963.	I was working at Claybury Mental Health Hospital, earning over £100 per month.	I began my training in nursing, which lasted for 3 years.

Date	Address / Accommodation	Event	Work	Notes
Mid-1963–1964	Angel, Islington, N1 Terraced house, private rental, a bedsit with shared facilities. Caribbean landlord owned the property.	I left the hospital living quarters but remained in my job. I was living with this Christian family called the Scotts.	Continued to work at Claybury Hospital.	I was attending a Pentecostal Church in Whiteland Street, Islington N1. This is how I came to know the Scott family.
1964–1965	Powerscroft Road, Clapton E5 A bedsit in a terraced property. A Trinidadian private landlord.	This is when the trouble began because I became pregnant with my son and so needed a bigger place; the room we were renting was too small. We would see advertisements for a room or two rooms, but by the time we got there, it would be gone. Then we began to become more aware of the racial divide. We saw the signs saying, "No blacks, no Irish, and no dogs." Therefore, you were often forced to rent from your own people.		The traditional English churches at that time were not so accepting of Caribbean families. I can recall that my husband tried to attend an Anglican Church and was turned away by the priest, who said that his presence would cause the congregation to diminish. Due to this, a lot of Caribbeans began to set up their own churches.
1965–1966	Antill Road, Tottenham, N15 A 2-room flat, shared accommodation. It was a private rental.	I was expecting my daughter.		I started to run the pardner with my work colleagues as we all used to get paid monthly. I used to be the banker and be responsible for collecting the money. This was a useful way of saving money.
1966–1967	Southwold Road, Clapton, Road E5 A 2-room flat owned by my husband's nephew.	I was expecting again. The property was owned by my husband's nephew, who was very anxious for us to come and live in the property. But it turned out to be a bad move. My husband's nephew was not nice, and in the end, we left that property after a falling out.		The flat was self-contained and furnished. We used to punch the gas, but when the rebate would come, my husband's nephew would take the money, saying that it was his property.
1967–1968	4 Dunn Street, Hackney E8 A 2-bedroom terraced house rented from a Jewish Man.	There were only two properties on the road, and across the road there were factories and shops.	Started working at Friern Hospital, which is commonly referred to as Friern Barnet Hospital as it was based in Barnet. I worked there until my retirement in 1993.	By this time, I had brought over to the England all six of my existing children, who were born in Jamaica. This was a gradual process over the years.

70a Darnley Road, Hackney E8 3-bedroom terraced house with an attic room.	1968–1973	Many of us in the family, one of my daughters in particular, voiced strongly that this house was haunted. Noises could be heard in the night but not from any member of family within the household. Footsteps of someone running across the hall were also heard. Family members on different occasions spoke of being pressed down whilst in their beds at night and being unable to speak. I had my son and youngest child in 1970.	
Mount Pleasant Lane, Hackney E5 We lived in a 5-bedroom terraced council house which we later were able to purchase through the Right to Buy scheme.	1973–1987	Being given the opportunity to purchase our own home through the Right to Buy is the only thing that I am grateful to Margaret Thatcher for ... If it was not for the fact that women did not have much of a say back in those days, then I would have been able to make more headway. This made it hard to progress. For instance, a woman could not go to the store and use credit to purchase anything; it had to be your husband. Things didn't really start to improve for women until the late 1970s–1980s.	There was a fire in the property due to the paraffin heater accidentally turning over and setting the place alight. Luckily, no one was hurt.
St Loys Road, Tottenham, N17 A 3-bedroom terraced house. Bought outright.	1987–present	One of my housing aspirations that hasn't come to fruition is to build a children's home back in Jamaica.	It took me 21 years to go back to Jamaica after leaving in 1961; I didn't go back until 1982. A lot of us have ended up with arthritis, I think due to the cold weather and living in properties without any heating in the early days, when we first arrived in this country.

Caribbean Women's Migration: *Windrush* Housing Experiences and Aspirations

Housing History since Arrival in the UK, Interviewee 5, from 1958 to 01.02.2014

Location/Tenure Type	Year/Duration	Experiences: Main Events Happening at the Time	Employment—Job Title/Role	Social Networks, Family, Friends, School, Work, Church
Riversdale Road, Finsbury Park, N4 A 3-storey property with basement. A private rental with a Jamaican landlord. All the tenants, except us, were Jamaican. We were the only Guyanese tenants living there.	February 1958–May 1958	I was 19 years old when I left Guyana to come to the UK. It cost $20 to travel from Guyana to Barbados and then £65 from Barbados to London, Victoria. My husband sent for me, and we were living in a rented room. We were living on the first floor. Four of us had to share the kitchen. There were two stoves, and we had to punch the gas. We suspected that the landlord was going into our room after we left and searching through our belongings. I would notice that our things were a little out of place or a bit ruffled, but I couldn't prove it. So, one day I came home early, sneaked in quietly, covered up in the bed, and waited. And sure enough, the landlord let himself in. He got a fright when I suddenly jumped up from the bed; he tried to make excuses, but I told him that as we were paying for our privacy, he should wait until we came home if he needed to access our room for anything. After this incident, we decided to move out.	My first job was in a sweet factory, Voile & Worley, working from 8 a.m. to 5 p.m. Pay was £5 per week. If you were 5 minutes late, they would deduct a quarter-hour pay. They would give you 3 minutes grace. It was hard work because of the heavy lifting involved. Large trays had to be lifted into the ovens, and I was little in frame. They used to call you "niggers" and "wogs", and you never had any rights.	In those days, your parents had to write a letter of consent in order to be able to travel to the UK. The age of consent at that time was 21 years, so my mother signed for me. We made acquaintances with other Guyanese people from back home. The supervisor was white and would give me all the dogs' body jobs. If you tried to stand up for your rights, they would sack you.

Location	Year		
Queens Drive, Finsbury Park, N4 A 3-storey building with a Jewish live-in landlord. It was a private rental bedsit with shared facilities.	1958–1959	I got married in October 1958. At first it was a struggle. I couldn't get a job easily as I was pregnant. And once they realised that, they would turn me down. Three months after my first child was born, I got a job. I had to get a nanny to babysit. We lived on the second floor of a bedsit. We had a cooker in the room, and we shared the toilet and the bath. The bathroom was used for everything, washing the dishes and ourselves. Had to punch the gas for cooking on the stove and electric for the light, and we used paraffin heaters to stay warm. The landlord decided to sell the property, so we had to move.	Laundromat, Caledonian Road N7 I didn't stay there long because I fell pregnant with my second daughter.
Queens Drive, Finsbury Park, N4. A bedsit with shared facilities in a 3-storey building. A private rental with a Jewish landlord.	1959–1960	The previous landlord put us on to another landlord, so we were able to move to another property on the same road. I had my second child. This landlord didn't live in the property but let out all of the rooms. We had one room and shared the kitchen and bathroom.	
Wray Crescent, Hornsey N8 Terraced house with basement. We lived in a small room on the top floor. A Jamaican woman was the landlady.	1960–1960	My husband and I decided it was best for me to return home to Guyana, where I had my third child. I stayed in Guyana for about 6 months before returning. I ended up leaving my two toddlers there and brought the baby back with me. It was the hardest thing that I had to do. They were there for two years, which was hard for me and them. My children were only meant to spend six months. I gave my husband the money to pay their fares while I was at work, but he kept saying it was too expensive, and he didn't pay their fares. The Jamaican landlady said she didn't want children living there, so we didn't stay long.	Later I was to find out that my husband had met a woman before he sent for me and had been staying with her at this address in my absence. His friends knew but never told me at the time; I only found out later, once I had all my children. His friends later said that they felt awkward to tell me. I had to get stronger and do things myself. It was not easy.

Graham Road, Clapton E5 We lived in a basement flat.	1960–1961		I had to give my husband all my money that I worked for. My husband worked with London Transport all the time he was living in England.
Albion Road, Stoke Newington, N16 Basement apartment in a 3-storey house.	1961–1962	Brought the children back from Guyana. I had my fourth child, that was a home birth. The social worker came to visit us, and I began to discuss my housing dilemma. We thought she might be able to help us, but she said that there were no places available on the council for people like us; we would need to be on the council waiting list for many years.	Worked in a factory making components for televisions. We had to wear protective clothing because we were handling acid. Earned £7 per week.
Powerscroft Road, Finsbury Park, N4 A 1-bedroom flat in a terraced house with sitting tenant. We went on to buy this property. Mortgaged.	1962–1975	We used the kitchen diner area as another bedroom and put in bunk beds. We had the living room area for our family and guest area. We barely got through with this place as the agent took our money, so we just moved in without any keys. We were polite and managed to get a key cut from the sitting tenant. It was a cheap property to buy because no one wanted to buy a property with a sitting tenant. My husband also was not keen at first, but I was tired of being forced to move from place to place with the children and wanted some stability. I told my husband that we needed to take a chance.	Worked as a childminder... Was an orderly at Hackney Hospital. I got sick and left. Worked in a factory making baby seats and car seat coverings in Hackney.
Radley Road, Tottenham, N17 A semi-detached 3- bedroom house. Bought outright.	1975–present	My last (fifth) child was born in this property. I got a childminder to help out with my youngest child. I have made quite a lot of improvements to the house over the years and opened up the space to make a good-sized kitchen diner. I recently made my upstairs bathroom bigger and updated it.	Still working at the baby seat factory when I first moved to this address.

Caribbean Women's Migration: *Windrush* **Housing Experiences and Aspirations**

Housing History since Arrival in the UK, Interviewee 6, from 1957 to 09.02.2014				
Location/ Tenure Type	Year/ Duration	Experiences: Main Events Happening at the Time	Employment— Job Title/Role	Social Networks, Family, Friends, School, Work, Church
Back Church Lane, Stepney EC1 Basement room in a 3-storey house. Private rental with shared accommodation and facilities.	One week in September 1957.	I left the Caribbean not knowing where I was going. I was following my cousin; she was coming to meet her partner. I didn't know if it were possible to go with her. Meanwhile, I met a man in my hometown who told me his brother had a property in the UK with rooms to let. This arrangement was appealing as my cousin was travelling on to Birmingham to meet with her partner. This allowed me to stay on in London. I sailed on the *Askania*. I paid £150 for my fares to England. An epidemic broke out on the ship, and we all got sick; it was a very unpleasant voyage with rough seas. We stopped off in Spain; after this, it began to get very cold. I was not used to feeling so cold. We arrived in Southampton before travelling on to London, where we were staying in the basement of this property. This frightened me. I had never seen a basement before. It was a large room with 5 single beds, and to my surprise, the man I travelled with introduced me as his girlfriend. There were five men staying in the basement, and I was the only woman. His brother never had any house; he was one of the tenants. I said to my so-called friend, "You lied to me." I was told that I had to sleep in one of the single beds with him, so I told him that I would sleep on the inside of the bed next to the wall, but if he touched me that I would kill him. There was only one washroom for all of us to use, so I asked the men to vacate the area when I needed to wash as there were no curtains ... no privacy. A friend heard of my situation and came to collect me, and from there I came to be living in Hackney.	I worked at a place where they made costume jewellery; I did the soldering. I was used to this as I did crafts back home in Dominica. I was earning £4 per week, but if I worked on Saturdays and Sundays, then I could earn £6.	Back home in Dominica, we had a family sewing business, and we had teachers in the family. The morning after my arrival to the UK and the basement property in London, the brother took me to the social security. I started working at a jewellery store the day after that. In England it was difficult getting from one place to another because it was very foggy all the time, so I tried to use buildings as landmarks until I got used to the fog.

Hackney E5, near Victoria Park. £2 per week for rent and I had to put 2 shillings in the gas which lasted a week.	1957–1959	Shared a room with the lady friend who rescued me. I got a room in the same building because her room was a single room, and when she had the baby, it was inconvenient. I met my husband and ended up getting married whilst at this property. He was someone who I had already met back home in Dominica, and he happened to know my friend who lived in my building, although none of us knew beforehand the connection. He would visit my friend, but I was always in my room. One day he came, and I opened the door, and I said, "What are you doing here?" he said, "Well, I live around the corner, and I'm visiting a friend." So, we started courting until eventually we got married.	Continued to work at the jewellery shop.	My friend was expecting a baby, so I helped her. When she was in hospital, I would bring her night things, and I helped her when she had the baby. England was strange with strange habits. My friend asked for salt fish in the shops and was told that they only sell bacon and eggs. Now this is everywhere and expensive.
Hackney E5 Same street/ location as above but different house.	1959–1960	My son was born in this property. Only once was I met with blatant racism. I boarded a bus, and I didn't have any change, only a £5 note, so I handed it to the conductress, who said, "You blacks like to show off your money", to which I replied, "Only because we don't like to waste it at the pub." As I was getting off the bus, the white conductress gave me one whack on the back of my shoulder, and I spun round and hit her with my umbrella.		All these houses only had outside toilets, and you had to go to the public baths once a week. When you came in, you paid, and you had a certain amount of hot water, so you had to mix it with cold. If you were not satisfied, then you gave more money, and you could top up the hot water. Because of the smog, the water got dirty quickly. You went to the bag wash, and the clothes were washed in the bag and dried in the bag because they were put in a big vat. Life was difficult; it was no bed of roses. Jobs were easy, but they were cheap. They used to have signs saying, "No Coloureds, no Irish, no dogs, and no babies", as this would make it so difficult to rent. Also, when you rented a room, the bed linen was filthy and the blankets as well. There was one cooker on the landing.

The border between Hackney and Bow E3 A 2-bedroom house which we bought but later realised that it was a leasehold.	1960–1967	Life was different. Bread was left outside and the milk was left outside. And the coalman came into the house with the coal in a bag over his shoulder, and he would place it under the stairs. It was so cold there was icicles hanging outside the window. You had a paraffin heater. You needed a partner; you needed to get married to lessen the pressure. The nappies were hanging on the rack in front of the paraffin heater, but you needed the heater to keep warm. I cried a lot every night. Seeing what I left behind where I had everything and it was hot made me sad. Back home you could wash in the river and dry your clothes in the sun. My little girl died at thirteen months. She got a cold, fell ill, and died suddenly. But my neighbours were very kind, and most of them were white. It was very hard for me being in a new country. I never had any brothers or sisters; I had a few cousins living outside of London. We had paid a deposit of £800 privately for this property; we thought we were buying a freehold property. It was a big blow for us when we got a letter from the leaseholder to say that the property was going to be demolished because he was selling it to a property developer. Eventually we were given a council flat in Manor House.	Where I lived in Bow, they called it the "little island" because there was only one way in and one way out. It was a very close-knit community, and meanwhile, three other Caribbean families moved in, one from St Vincent and two other families from Dominica. Those were happier times. My neighbours were very supportive; when my little girl died; they were all there for me, and most were white. Their children played with mine.
Manor House, N4 A 3-bedroom council flat.	1967–1969	By then I was having my third child. I got very sick during the labour and was not well for some time. It took time for me to recover.	I was unable to work.
Woodside Gardens, Tottenham, N17 A 3-bedroom property bought outright.	1969–present	In 1994, my husband died in my arms of an asthma attack. We did a lot of work on this property when we bought it. It had an outside toilet that we brought inside, and we made other renovations.	I went into the caring profession which helped me to heal. I have travelled back and forth to Dominica many times with my children. I would like to go back for the last time this year due to my age and because the journey is tedious. We have to stop over in Antigua and take a small plane from there over to Dominica.

Caribbean Women's Migration: *Windrush* Housing Experiences and Aspirations

Housing History since Arrival in the UK, Interviewee 7, from 1950 to 13.02.2014

Location/Tenure Type	Year/Duration	Experiences: Main Events Happening at the Time	Employment— Job Title/Role	Social networks, family, friends, School, Work, Church
Brightling Road, Brockley, SE4 A 3-bedroom semi-detached house. Landlords were a Canadian and English couple.	November 1950–1951	It was freezing cold when I arrived. I travelled on a ship called the *Rena Dell Pacifica*. It was a tourist ship with different sections such as first class, standard class, and so on. A baby girl was born on the ship, and she was named Rena Dell. I was supposed to be landing at Liverpool. I came with my friend, but I did not like the behaviour on the ship, so I decided to come off at Plymouth, where my sister's husband came to meet me. The nice thing was that this house actually had a bathroom inside, so I did not need to go to the public baths. My rent was 15 shillings per week, that soon doubled to 30 shillings as I was using a lot of water. But I didn't mind as this was a luxury in those days. When I arrived in England, everything was on rations; you had your ration book. Cheese, butter, eggs (I was given 1 egg for the baby), sugar, and things like tea were all on rations. Sweets were rationed; the first fortnight you were allowed a quarter pound of sweets, and the second fortnight you'd get a half pound. You were allowed a slice of beef and a slice of corned beef for the week. You could go to the Jewish to get chicken, and rabbit was also available, but I could not get used to the rabbit and stopped eating it.	I was a live-in nanny. I looked after the couple's baby that I was living with. I worked with the Jewish community in the rag trade, earning: £5 per week in White Chapel.	My mother was part German. She died when I was 3 years old, so I only have a very vague memory of her. When she died, my sister and I got separated. She went to her father, and I went to mine. We did not reunite until I was 16 years old. My sister had a better memory of our mother as she was five years older than I. When I first arrived, I started attending St Andrew's Church in Brockley Rise. I had been going there for three weeks. Then on the last occasion, the vicar took me aside and told me that he would appreciate it if I did not return anymore as there had been a notable drop in the congregation, and in the end, it was a matter of figures. So, with that said, I did not return. I then joined the brethren denomination, which I was familiar with from back home in Jamaica.

			When I went to Stella Fisher's Employment Bureaux in the Strand, they put me to do a typing test, but I said that I didn't finish my training in Jamaica, so I would not be up to the standard. So, they asked me if I would be happy to do filing, and I said yes. I enjoyed my job, and I was the only Jamaican there. There were a Trinidadian lady and a Dutch lady, apart from the English staff, of course. I was given the opportunity to go to college to do a typing course. I went on to become a secretary to the boss.
		Filing clerk, Phillips Electrical, Gramophone Section, in Marble Arch opposite Park Lane. I got the opportunity to meet some stars when they came to the recording studio, such as: Liberace—American pianist who was very funny and very flamboyant. The Kaye Sisters—British trio of pop singers. Frankie Vaughn—English singer. Frankie Valli and the Four Seasons—American singer/group. Shirley Bassey—Welsh singer.	
Blackheath Hill, border of Greenwich and Lewisham A flat in a 3-bedroom terraced house. My sister was the landlady.	1951–1952	I had my first child. A friend helped me to find a nanny to care for my baby. I went back to work when my baby was three months old. Nanny was an English lady who would become a lifelong friend. She went on to care for all of my children. No black people were on the buses; they wouldn't ever employ blacks on the bus then. The conductors used to help lift the pram on to the bus back then, but when they saw that the baby was black, they did not want to help. But Nanny insisted that they pick up the pram; she said it was their job to do so. When my daughter started school, she was the only black child … She suffered a lot of racism from the other children. When Nanny realised this, she would go and collect her from school, take her home for lunch, and then take her back afterwards. When I first came, you couldn't get any Caribbean provisions, such as cod fish. Gradually, things started to come through Brixton market. You asked for things, and they would say that they would try to get it. Then it would come over on the banana boat. There weren't many cars about because the metal had been used to make ammunition for the war.	
Wood Vale, Peckham, SE15 A bedsit in a 3-storey house with shared facilities. A Polish woman was the landlady.	1952–1953	I got married in January 1952, and it snowed. I was expecting, so I had to move as the landlady wasn't keen to continue allowing me to rent with another child on the way. You had to punch a penny for the bath.	Secretary working at London Bridge for 13 years.

	1953–1953	Fourth-floor flat, which I had to walk up … Under the windowsill there were holes because of the bombings. I had to stuff paper in the holes to help keep the draught out.	
9 Walden Shore Road, Forest Hill, SE 23 Private rental.			English people were not really buying properties at this time. They started building flats. That's what became the in thing.
7 Walden Shore Road, Forest Hill, SE 23 A mortgaged home.	1953–1958		I started to run pardners as this enabled us Caribbeans to help each other to buy our own houses; most times, this was the only way we could get properties to buy. My son went on to buy this property from his dad. If things had been different, we could have owned a few properties.
Devonshire Road, Forest Hill, SE23 A double-front terraced house for which we were able to get a mortgage.	1958–1989	This house had a huge garden with a train line at the back … The children went to Jamaica for 6 months; my husband sent them there so that he could get on with his studies uninterrupted. I was working all the time, which mean that on occasions, he would have to collect the children from school and take care of them … Nanny paid the fares to bring them back, and afterwards, I reimbursed her. We paid three and a half thousand pounds for the house. This house had two kitchens, two bathrooms, and a shower. There were only four houses like ours on the whole street. When we bought the house, my name was not on the freehold because in those days, women had no rights, so the man had all the power. And although my money was invested in the property, even more than my husband's—because he was always studying—by law, I didn't have any rights. Therefore, he was later able to sell the property from under me without me having any say.	

Property	Dates	Narrative	Work	Notes
Perry Rise, Forest Hill, Border of Sydenham, SE23 Semi-detached 3-bedroom house. A mortgaged property.	1989–2009	My marriage became strained after moving from Devonshire Road. I was very unhappy about leaving this house.	I worked until I was 73 years old. I was working for Southwark Council doing home care up until I retired.	My husband went on to become the mayor of Lewisham, but he held the post for just one year.
Devonshire Road, Forest Hill, SE23	2009–2012	I went to live with my son until he sold the house and paid my husband what he owed him for the house.		
Thornford Road, Lewisham, SE1 A 3-bedroom house. A mortgaged property.	2012- Present.	I live with my daughter now and have had an outside shed built to accommodate my things … I have a property in Jamaica which I try to go and stay at as often as I can. I am thinking of renting it out in the future. I have had many offers to buy it as it is in a sought-after location, but I am not interested to sell.		I continue to run a pardner scheme; I thought about packing it in, but the people that are in it don't want me to. Plus, it keeps my brain active. I continue to do caring in the community as a volunteer. There is a lady I go and visit every other day; she is blind. I cook for her and do her shopping and ironing. My legs are not as strong as they used to be, but I will continue for as long as I can.

Caribbean Women's Migration: *Windrush* **Housing Experiences and Aspirations**

Housing History since Arrival in the UK, Interviewee 8, from 1948 to 26.02.2014			
Location/Tenure Type	Year/ Duration	Experiences: Main Events Happening at the Time	Employment– Job Title/Role	Social Networks, Family, Friends, School, Work, Church
220 Brockley Road. Brockley, SE4 Private rental bedsit accommodation. An Englishwoman was the landlady.	1948–1950	Before I arrived, my husband was staying in a hostel in Camberwell Green. He came in 1947 on a ship called the *Almansora*. When my husband left me, I was 7 months pregnant. I came by ship, the *Orbita*, in September 1948. I was supposed to come on the *Windrush*, but I could not secure a ticket. The weather was bad. They screwed down the plates so that they didn't move when you're eating … my things is running over to you, and yours to me according to how the boat was rocking. I docked at Liverpool, and then got a train I left my two sons in Jamaica. We had a room. They had a little conservatory that would take you out into the garden. An old English lady lived upstairs, and she had a bath. But you couldn't use it; she had control of the house, and she had the best area. But it was for her use only. We had to go to the public baths. In those days, the seasons were more accurate. When it was winter, it was winter, and spring was spring. And summer was nice and hot. When I went to work, she had a daughter who would go in my room and take my things. They had a neighbour who she would talk with.	I was a metal worker for Francis Sheet Metal, I made the petrol cans. we had to test them in the water to see if they were leaking. I was paid £3 to 4 per week. It was a nice place, and you paid a shilling or one and six pence towards what they called a "bino" to go on trips such as to the seaside, Margate.	They had trams then, but not like the ones today. It was lovely. While one was going up, one would be going down. We would take it from here to New Cross Way … You would have the coalman who would draw the coal by horse and cart. You'd get coal in big bags. They'd hold the coal at an angle, and the coal would go down into the cellar. There were no motor cars then. You never saw them.

I used to work for Charlie Kray, not knowing who he actually was at the time. We didn't see him often, but we knew he owned the factory where I learnt my trade as a machinist for ladies' costumes and coats. He was a gentleman. He would come around once in a blue moon, and when he came, he would always carry Jewish cakes and such, and all the workers would get some. He was a rogue with other people, but he wasn't a rogue to us. You would hear whispering, "Charlie is here." [Interviewee 8 begins to sing the" Sugar Bush Song". It was a popular song in those days.] Those days you had some sad stories. Mrs Fitz (white, European) did cleaning where I worked in the clothes factory. She was married to a little African man, and he was an angel. She had two sons, no daughters. One son had a daughter, and as you looked at her, you could see that she was half caste. She had a baby and got married and quickly had another baby; the baby girl looked like a black baby, and her husband (who was white) swore it was not his baby. The marriage broke up, and he divorced her. When something happened and the child had to have a blood test, and it's through the blood test that they found out that the child was the husband's. He treated her so badly. The divorce went through, but when he found out the truth, he wanted to remarry her, but she said no. She was everything like her mother, so lovely and passive.

The landlady would point her finger and gossip about me to her neighbour. They'd ask about the Caribbean and take the piss. Like one day I washed and was hanging my washing on the line when they began questioning me, and I was answering. They continued to ask what I did when I was in Jamaica, and I turned and said I used to swing from tree to tree, like a monkey. After that, they never asked me no question again. In the end they gave my husband notice to go, even though I had the baby. When I came, there was open land everywhere and lots of rubble; you wouldn't have to walk far. You'd see derelict buildings from the bombings. Those days you were poor. Rations were the only way you got some food and clothes. You couldn't buy eggs unless they were cracked and only if you were pregnant. You couldn't get meat; it was only corned beef and I didn't eat that, so I would give it to someone. Meat would be maybe once a month, and it would be a very small portion. We'd leave our ration book over by the grocery shop to make sure we got something. Times were hard, but you got by. If you used your ration coupon to buy bread or sweets, then you couldn't get any sugar. Coming from the West Indies, I had a sweet tooth, so we were told of a Jewish man in Chadwell where we'd get a two-pound bag of sugar for four shillings on the black market down the East End. That's how I got to work in the men's and women's clothing trade—Costume Mantel ... Women didn't wear trousers then. It was tweed called goray that we would wear in the winter.

Address	Dates		
		In 1951, there was a hurricane out in Jamaica; I took the baby home to Jamaica, and a storm broke out about a week or so after. Because of the storm, I couldn't get a boat or anything to bring me back over to England. That baby died in Jamaica. Also, when I travelled home with the baby, I was already pregnant again but didn't know at the time. Later that year, after I returned to England to my husband, we had an argument and went to bed. A little afterwards, I felt a kick, and because we were lying head to foot, I thought that my husband stretched out his foot and kicked me. I went to the doctor, as he was near to where I lived, and he said I was pregnant and sent me to Greenwich Hospital. They said I was seven months pregnant. I couldn't believe it. My third baby, that I took to Jamaica, died. My fourth baby, a girl, was born exactly one year and a day later. When I first came to the UK, people weren't going to church. The Catholic Church I went to was dismal and dark, and they barely had any congregation. Everything was done in Latin.	I was in a pardner. I still am. We couldn't do nothing without a pardner.
Honor Oak Park, Forest Hill, SE4 A shop was round the side. It was an upstairs house. The landlady was a nice English lady. She had 4 boys and 1 girl. She was a florist.	1951–1952	I went to Jamaica and took the baby in 1950; I returned in 1951, leaving baby with my mum. I came back to find out I was expecting again. When I moved into the property with my little baby, the landlady's youngest son said, "Look, Mummy, the baby is black all over." When the Queen had her coronation in 1952, she and her husband, Prince Phillip, went to Africa. Then she was told her father died and had to come back. At the time, I was working at New Road, White Chapel, and we stood by the hospital. We begged to go out, and we promised to work back the time. They drove very, very slowly, and you could see her face close up. You could run and meet up with her it was that slow. She was beautiful, so lovely. I also went to see King George VI lying in state. You didn't see him actually; you only saw the coffin. My dad came over from Jamaica to live in the UK. I played a prank on him. I hid the landlady's dog, Skipper, and the dog jumped out on him. My dad loved dogs, like me, and we had dogs back home in Jamaica; but my mum didn't.	
104 Talford Road, Peckham, SE15 We lived in a 3-bedroom house which we bought with a mortgage.	1952–1958	This house had a big bathroom, kitchen, and garden. It was my husband and brother-in-law that did business, but we had more money in it than they did. When we sold that house, we went straight back to Brockley. I loved Brockley. My last child was born there. My landlady from Honour Oak Park crocheted my baby girl's christening gown. We became friends.	
45 Upper Brockley Road, Brockley, SE4 A 3-bedroom terraced house with a basement we bought with an extension.	1958–1963	In December 1963, my two eldest sons came from Jamaica to live with us.	

Manor Avenue, SE4, off Lewisham Way, near New Cross Station. We had the top half of a big house. There was no bathroom. Sitting tenants lived in the bottom half of the house.	1963–1965	My father was ill. He lived in Brunswick Road.		
Aspinal Road, SE4, behind Brockley Station. A semi-detached, 4-bedroom house with a big living room area.	1965–1967	My marriage broke down, and we sold this property. I decided to go to the States and stayed with my family over there.	I setup a hairdressing parlour in my house and worked from home.	
Gloucester Road, Croydon, CRO 2DE I lived in a halfway house.	1967–1968	I left my daughter with the childminder. The boys stayed with me, and I went to America for a little over a year (1968–1969). My family wanted me to stay permanently. When I returned, I bought Westbury Road. My dad and I were very close, and he was drinking more heavily than before, so I returned. He died at the Prince of Wales Hospital. Tottenham, N15 [now closed].		My husband bought another property; we lived separately.
Westbury Road, Croydon A 3-bedroom, semi-detached house. Bought outright	1969–present	This house is about 120 years old.	I worked at Cane Hill Mental Hospital until retirement. It has been closed.	I started attending St Mary's Catholic Church. An African pastor is there now.

CHAPTER 5

Case-Study Review: An Analysis of the Findings

The primary research case study about Caribbean women's individual historical tenure experience is identified using a mixed methods research approach to compare, contrast, and accentuate recurrent themes applicable to the early period after they arrived. Prevalent social attitudes identifiable to the black Caribbean migration experience are revealed, reminiscent of Britain in a different era.

Key Findings

(1)   Housing

(2)   Jobs

(3)   Education

(4)   Social Factors

(1) Housing

Relating to location and settlement patterns, all the women, some for over three decades, have stayed within a five- to 10-mile radius of where they lived when they first arrived in the United Kingdom. Except for one, all have been living in their current or last mortgaged property for a minimum of twenty-seven years. Three have resided in their present home since 1969, amounting to forty-five years at the time of the study.

Women's Case-Study Housing Summary

On arrival to the United Kingdom, the women lived in private rental multi-occupancy housing, usually in one room. A few of the women experienced having no choice but to share with strangers. All of the women with the exception of Interviewee 7, attended public baths; having a bath in a rented property was a luxury. The women explained that they would have to "punch" the gas and electric. There was no such thing as security of tenure in those days, and women discussed the fact that they were forced to move frequently. This situation worsened with more children as landlords preferred not to rent to couples with children. MacEwen (1991), surmises that research published in 1975 showed the data findings from ten local authorities revealed ethnic disadvantage regarding eligibility for council housing as Caribbeans did not meet the criterion of priority on entry to the United Kingdom (Hamnett and Butler 2010: 57), coupled with discriminatory allocation practices (Phillips and Harrison 2010: 222).

Caribbeans were often not situated specifically in areas planned for slum clearance but in neighbouring areas. Also housing priority systems factored into the equation such things as lack of information and understanding of the council housing system, as well as overt racial bias. This left Caribbeans with limited choices other than to rent privately or to seek mortgaged home ownership of usually cheap and rundown properties, and according to research, in some cases with sitting tenants, making house purchases less desirable but also cheaper (Patterson 1965: 161–165). This also rendered Caribbeans ineligible to apply for council property (Macewen 1991: 64–66).

All the women except for the two earliest arrivals rented from landlords of Jewish or Caribbean ethnicity; Interviewees 7 and 8 rented from English landlords. Private rental was a lucrative business, and private landlords were unlegislated, meaning they could charge whatever rates they saw fit. Also, there were no health and safety regulations to adhere to (Lowe 2011: 93, 94; Lund 2011: 57).

Private agencies were often underhanded in their dealings and did not make the facts clear. This was the case with Interviewee 6, where she and her husband thought that they were paying a mortgage towards purchasing their own house, a freehold, only later to find out it was a leasehold. After paying their deposit, they were being informed by the leaseholder that the property was going to be demolished.

Revealingly, McEwen states that "Black owner-occupiers have frequently found access to mortgage finance restricted" (McEwen 1991: 16–19). Somerville and Steele refer to the point that "Estate agents operating discriminatory practices against BME groups have restricted owner-occupation to some BME groups and served to reinforce segregation in some geographical areas" (Somerville and Steele 2002: 163).

Property Ownership

All eight case-study women interviewed met the aspiration of becoming homeowners in the United Kingdom. Seven of the eight women, by eventually purchasing on the open property market. However, two women no longer own property in the United Kingdom. Both women have bought property in Jamaica but live with grown children as part of an extended family network in the United Kingdom. Both women no longer live with their husbands; one is divorced, and one is separated but civil with her husband. Only one of the case-study women later got on to the property ladder through Margaret Thatcher's Conservative housing policy right to buy scheme.

Housing Theory

Barn (2001) describes two theoretical perspectives, "choice and constraint". Choice theorists argue that geographical concentrations of black communities may be stimulated by a preference to live in areas that reflect their racial/cultural identities, support networks, religious affiliations, and dialects. In contrast, constraint theorists have argued that black Caribbean's persistent settlement patterns in racially segregated areas is attributable to fear, institutionally discriminatory housing practices, and economic level (Barn 2001: 10; Peach 1998; Phillips and Harrison 2010).

Both theories raise points worth considering and arguably, validity of what equates to the authentic value of choice. Harrison and Phillips (2003), highlight housing needs in terms of "commonality of community" and the inclination to retain familiar associations linked to community, memories, kinsfolk, friends, religion, culture, and cuisine. They also emphasise that these values become more imperative in later life.

Housing Acquisition and Pardner Schemes

All but one of the women actively engaged in throwing pardners. A few of the women were the bankers; it was expressed repeatedly how much of a financial lifeline it was. It was a commitment, and for most, it was the only way they could conceive of becoming homeowners. Pardners were a way for fellow Caribbeans to bond in solidarity over a common cause to elevate themselves and aspire to improve their socio-economic positions and gain stability for themselves and their families in the United Kingdom and abroad.

Pardner schemes were not just a cultural tradition that has been passed down through generations since slavery. It was and for Caribbeans today who use this method, it is a way of life. Because these mechanisms of community saving were transported from the Caribbean, Caribbeans often preferred this method to saving money in a bank. As explained by Interviewee 1, "This was a commitment we would make to ourselves … With a savings of five to six hundred pounds, you could get on the property ladder, even if you started off with a leasehold."

Interestingly, Interviewee 1 went on to say how after the war, white people lost interest initially in buying property because of the bombing of their properties during the war. Interviewee 7 also speaks of this, saying that English people were not buying property so much and that flats were the new thing.

The Growth of High-Rise Flats

The building of high-rise flats was inspired by the architectural design of Le Corbusier (international career: 1927–1945), that started to gain momentum for incorporating as part of new tenure construction, and new advancement in building technology which prior to the mid-fifties, was prevented due to limitations on building heights. This was no longer an issue by the 1960s. Lund (2011) contends that a series of housing surveys would consistently reveal that British working-class people overwhelmingly had not been in favour of high-rise flats. This was significant as it was the working-class masses who were destined to live in these buildings. But a government initiative for such buildings accelerated during 1966 and 1967. It is stated by Lund that of the percentage of buildings being constructed at this time, 25 per cent were high-rise, and in larger metropolitan cities, these percentages were much higher. These new and often industrialised building systems saw the rise of tower blocks by as much as 70 per cent in the Greater London regions.

Le Corbusier's "high modernism", backed by prominent architects of the day Peter and Alison Smithson, were inspired by this visionary model of "streets in the sky" and rebuffed the traditional ground-level terraced houses that people were accustomed to, proclaiming, "Folk-building is dead in England." The thought process originally behind Le Corbusier's high-rise flats was to provide, "well spaced tower blocks, providing homes with equal access to daylight, should be linked by 'streets in the air' to encourage social interaction and allow the areas around the blocks to be used as parkland" (Lund 2011: 59).

However, the growth of the high-rise stimulated via Labour housing initiatives from 1964 to 1970 would be seen as a notably unsuccessful policy strategy.

In spite of Caribbean housing dilemmas, it made sense that although faced with multiple challenges, Caribbeans also felt that coming to the United Kingdom presented them with a great opportunity that they desired to grasp on to. Patterson documents the general sentiment by white residents to black settlement: "In Brixton, for instance, there is a widespread belief that the arrival of coloured residents in a street or neighbourhood causes property values to depreciate. Our street is getting 'hot'—the blacks are beginning to move in, and we'll have to sell and move while the going's good" (Patterson 1965: 171).

Caribbean Landlords

Three of the women in the case study spoke of issues with Caribbean landlords. Interviewee 2 said that a Jamaican landlord purposely caused damage to the pipe under the kitchen sink after she left the property for a short time in order to use it as an excuse to evict her.

Interviewee 5 had suspicions that her Jamaican landlord was entering her and her husband's room when they left the house. She decided to come home early one day and hide. When the landlord entered, she revealed herself, much so his surprise. It was flagged up that her and her husband were the only occupants at that time who were not from Jamaica and, this also seemed to present an underlying issue, possibly for both parties, landlord and tenants. Caribbeans were often lumped together as if they were one group. Each Caribbean Island has its own national identity and pride and showed displeasure in being lumped together into one melting pot, so to speak. There were inter-island conflicts, bickering, and superiority complexes relating to island size. This mentality has a long history in the Caribbean.

Interviewee 4 recalled renting a two-bedroom flat from her husband's nephew (1966–1967), but it would lead to discord. It would appear from the account that it would become less about family and kinship support and more about making a profit.

(2) Jobs

In terms of the women's migration in relation to *Windrush* case-study findings, women's initial occupations on arrival to the United Kingdom found that four women—Interviewees 1, 3, 7, and 8—worked in the rag trade. Interviewee 8 also later set up her own hairdressing parlour in her home. Interviewees 2 and 5 worked in factories. Interviewee 4 worked in a canteen, and Interview 6 worked in a small company firm. These were the occupation categories typical of the jobs available to Caribbean migrants, poorly paid, menial, unskilled labour which white workers shunned (Sivanandan 1982: 103). Whites' undesirability for certain occupations would serve to create a racialised division of labour (Phillips 1998: 1682).

Male-Female Division of Labour

Four out of the eight case-study women worked in the rag trade, or clothing industry when they first arrived in the United Kingdom. Therefore, it seems fitting to look at this industry in order to formulate a clearer picture of the circumstances pertinent to that time.

The making of a garment by an individual skilled worker was referred to by the Board of Trade in 1947 as, "making through". At the time, males were responsible for stitching together the main body of the garment. The less-skilled operations— for example, the sewing of buttonholes and pockets—were completed by so-called assistants, who were men and women. The master tailor system was started by Jewish tailoring workshops. Under this operational system, the head tailor was normally contracted for the work and performed the skilled techniques of making the garment. He would be responsible for recruiting and employing the less-skilled assistant labour. This practice was also known as the "set system" and transferred over into factory production. In the factory setting, the head machinist was responsible for organising and supervising the bench of machinists. The production process was predominantly overseen by craftsmen who controlled the working activities and wages of the less-skilled workers.

After the war, most union agreements ended the use of the set system. There became a wider division of labour, and clothing produced in the United Kingdom became the labour of women working in small sweatshops or from home for very low rates of pay. The clothing industry after the war was de-skilled, meaning that comparisons between complex and simplified tasks were blurred, and men and women who once may have performed different jobs were now part of the same production process. With de-skilling instilled in the process, the sexual divisions in labour became more apparent. The mechanisation process turned garment making into a mass-production industry. The work became more competitive, but it was still required to be completed at high speed to meet management's production targets. Despite the technology of sewing machines, some details still needed to be performed with, "skill and judgement ... This is true of stitching of pockets, sleeves and collars, where the operator has to position and manipulate the fabric as it is stitched. These operations have a longer training period than other machining operation" (Coyle, cited in West 1982: 14–15).

According to Coyle, it would take up to six months on average to reach required production speeds, but this wasn't reflected in the wages. Women became employed in relation to the cheapening of labour and in competition with men: "The division of labour is not just a convenient separation of tasks but, 'divided and hostile' and men have always opposed and sought to restrict the conditions of women's employment. The development of capitalist production on the basis of gender divisions has meant that no workers' struggle has ever been free of these sexual politics" (West 1982: 23).

Male trade unionists sought to maintain the status quo by actively participating in control and resist tactics in the employment of women and in favour of the continuance of securing, "a larger bread winner's wage for men". (Coyle, cited in West, 1982: 24) Women were forced to defend their rights from being relegated to a subordinate position to men within the workforce. Although it was argued that working women could no longer be seen as being dependant on their husbands, their positioning in relation to men in practice was still inferior. Coyle assesses that "The only guarantee women have that their own interests will be considered is to organise as workers and as women" (Coyle, cited in West, 1982: 25).

Discriminatory Work Practices and Types of Employment Experienced by the Case-Study Women

The women's case-study research regarding incidences of discrimination in the workplace revealed two occurrences. Interviewee 2 experienced discrimination when she worked for Norman Stanley Estate Agents, doing accountancy work. The other was Interviewee 5, who worked in a sweet factory when she first arrived in the United Kingdom. She shared, "It was hard work because of the heavy lifting involved. Large trays had to be lifted into the ovens, and I was only little in frame. They used to call you 'niggers' and 'wogs', and you never had any rights."

Phillips (1998) points out that the government tended to disregard discriminatory processes prevalent in both the workforce and housing market during this post-war migration period. Over time, as women gained stability and progressed in housing, employment, and family life. And coupled with the natural processes of adaption and settlement; the gradual progression within the job market, along with the widening of the women's skill base, education and training, they were able to seek better and more fulfilling career paths. Some jobs, according to Interviewee 1, "had schemes where you pay in 'subs' so that the workers could go on trips to the seaside or theatre etc."

Interestingly, Interviewee 8 spoke of working for Charlie Kray, the eldest brother of the notorious Kray twins, Reggie and Ronnie, who resided in the East End. She described him as a "gentleman". At the time, she was working as a machinist for ladies' clothing, in a company owned by Charlie Kray. She explains, "He would come around once in a blue moon, but when he came, he would always carry Jewish cakes and such, and all the workers would get some. He was a rogue with other people, but he wasn't a rogue to us ... you would hear whispering, 'Charlie is here.'"

At one point in her employment history, Interviewee 7 worked as a filing clerk at Phillips Electrical, in the Gramophone Section, where she got to meet celebrities of the time, including Shirley Bassey, Liberace, the Kay Sisters, Frankie Vaughn, and Frankie Valli and The Four Seasons.

Last documented occupations of the migration/*Windrush* women:

- Interviewee 1: A teaching assistant in a secondary school for the Hackney Council Local Authority.

- Interviewee 2: Assistant supervisor in accounts.

- Interviewee 3: Manager, Camden Council Local Authority.

- Interviewee 4: Qualified mental health nurse.

- Interviewee 5: Factory worker.

- Interviewee 6: Worked in the caring profession.

- Interviewee 7: Worked for Southwark Council Local Authority as a care-home worker.

- Interviewee 8: Mental healthcare worker.

Patterson asserts that in regards to Britain as an importer of immigrant Labour, on arrival, securing a job and a roof over one's head would be the priority of the "newcomer" in Britain. At the same time housing and jobs, are also two main fields of competition that evoke feelings of antagonism and indignation towards the newcomers by the natives. Britain's countrywide history of discontent and discrimination against Irish, foreign, and coloured immigrants, in Patterson's opinion, relates to, "the degree of economic insecurity felt by the local working population". She goes further to use the example of, "the hostility and discrimination directed at Coloured seamen in Cardiff—that increased during the shipping industry's lean years from 1921 to 1938 and left an enduring mark on local attitudes, as highlighted by Dr Kenneth Little" (Patterson 1965: 61).

The black Cardiff seamen case is reverberated by Fryer and eventually provoked an investigation of the seamen's dire situation by two members of the League of Coloured Peoples in April 1935 and reported back to Harold Moody (Head founder of the League of Coloured Peoples). In addition to discrimination in employment, other issues discovered were,

> The shameful conditions in which Cardiff's black community was condemned to live … segregated them from the more salubrious quarters of the town … those living in such slums for the most part put their children's needs above their own … it is noteworthy that children of coloured men almost always appear well fed and are warmly dressed in spite of the poverty … Yet these children, when they left school, could never find work in a factory or an office, no matter their qualifications. (Fryer, 1984: 358)

(3) Education

Post-WWII Education in England and Wales

Interviewee 7 spoke about the racism that her daughter faced at school: "When my daughter started school, she was the only black child … She suffered a lot of racism from other children. When Nanny realised, she would collect her from school, take her home for lunch, then take her back afterwards." (See chapter 4.)

The 1944 Education Act was passed in England and Wales under a growing demand for educational improvements expressed during the Second World War. This would mark a fundamental milestone in the British education system with the announcing of free secondary education for all. The minister of education was empowered with the task as a matter of priority. Education was divided into three stages: primary (children five to twelve years old), secondary (pupils twelve to fifteen years old, raised to sixteen years old in 1947), and lastly, compulsory part-time education for young people aged fifteen to seventeen in the county colleges.

In addition, church schools were brought closer in line with state educational practices and protocols. The local authorities provided social service provisions such as free milk, affordable meals, and medical inspection, along with free medical and dental care. Naturally, there was to be a sharp rise of pupils seeking access to the free schooling entitlement for all, and it outstripped school buildings' availability. The rebuilding of schools begun in 1948.

However, it is important to note that during the early post-war years in the United Kingdom, housing and industry competed with education for the country's limited building resources. By the 1950s, England was experiencing a baby boom which made the construction of schools for all three stages a necessity (Johnson, Whyman, and Wykes 1968: 170, 171).

(4) Social Factors: Experiences, Family, Lifestyle, and Cultural Identity

Family Structure in the Caribbean and the United Kingdom

Ellis (1986: 7) illustrates that family-type groupings in the Caribbean are intricate and varied. You have the Western patriarchal nuclear family, the female-centred matriarchal family, the extended family setting, and the single-parent family (typically woman-headed) that can be found at all economic levels of Caribbean society. There are also family members who do not all live in the same household. This correlates with Interviewee 3's family situation, where she said that she came, "from a family of ten; three of us lived with my paternal grandmother. My mother and father were never married but lived very close to one another, so I saw my mother all the time. It could be likened to an extended family situation." She went on to say that despite her mother and father living in separate dwellings and the children being divided between both parents' homes, "the father's ruling took priority."

Marriage

In discussing the subject of marriage, Ellis (1986: 7) elaborates that in the case of mature women and couples in lower socio-economic positions, marriage was perceived as equating to an improved lifestyle and household income. Indeed, many of the case-study women expressed that it was beneficial, even necessary, especially as women had less rights accorded to them.

"You needed a partner, you needed to get married to lessen the pressure." (Interviewee 6)

Interviewee 1 shared a similar sentiment:

"I met the man who was to become my husband ... in the end because of our limited earnings and wanting to be more stable, we ended up deciding to live together in order to pool resources and ease the strain."

Poverty, hardship, and the stigma of having children out of wedlock facilitated early marriages. Being a couple helped to ease financial burdens and the mental anguish of facing problems alone, without the support of family and kinship ties. And for women, it gave them respectability.

Miscegenation

During the case-study interview, discussions relating to racial intermixing came about as was also pinpointed during Sheila Patterson's study of black Caribbeans in Brixton in her book *Dark Strangers* (1965); see section 2.1—page 12.

The 1948 interviewee 8, spoke of an interracial marriage that ended in divorce due to suspicions of infidelity on the part of the wife, who herself was of interracial ethnicity, and her husband was white. This suspicion arose from the fact that one of their children was born with a darker complexion. But in the end, it would be confirmed that the child was not born of adultery and was biologically the husbands. The story gives rise to the social complexities and obvious racialized stigma attached to interracial unions prevalent at the time.

School Teacher and Author, Beryl Gilroy was married to a white Englishman. She was a devoted wife and mother, although she expresses anxiousness of the British society in which she lived, her new home; that Gilroy also confessed had "*conditioned her way of thinking,*" Gilroy confronts her fears in Black Teacher:

> I had to be the perfect housewife and perfect mother. I must be above all possible white criticism ... I worried, too, about my child to be - the product of what was called 'miscegenation'. It wasn't its colour or the texture of its hair that bothered me, but its wholeness. (Gilroy, 1994: 109)

Caribbean Men and Women in Relationships

Following extensive case studies of Caribbean society and cultural perspective analysis, Pat Ellis (1986) concluded that male-female relationships, including marriages, are complex and contradictory. Men and women have been given mixed and conflicting messages about how to behave in a relationship. For instance, girls are taught from an early age how to be resourceful. They are taught to cook, clean, care for, and organise in preparation for a family and husband, whether this materialises in her life or not. This teaching helps to foster inner strength and independence. It also gives credence to the imagery of the strong black woman who has the resilience to overcome and withstand everything and anything. Although contrary to this, she is also taught that it is advantageous and looked on favourably to have a husband, and she should adhere to her spouse's wishes. Being able to balance the scales of responsibility, independence, and marital status is likened to reaching the pinnacle of womanhood. (Ellis, 1986: 8)

Similarly with young men, they, too, receive mixed messages about how to conduct themselves when transitioning from boys to men. They are often not guided or pushed to be as independent or responsible as girls. Nor are they taught the necessary survival or practical skills to manage a home and be self-sufficient. As a result, men are often more likely to be reliant on their mothers, sisters, and other female relatives, and later, partners and wives. Although there is a cultural behaviour pattern and way of thinking that the man should be the one to exert a dominant role in the relationship, this can lead to men feeling an underlying resentment of their reliance on their wives or partners. That learnt pattern of behaviour is a familiar trait in Caribbean male-female relationship dynamics. Left unaddressed, it inevitably gives rise to confusion, discontent, and resentment, leading to turbulent or even violent relationships that are destructive to family life: "Children see their strong mothers experiencing oppression and showing insecurity as they relate to their male partners and this cycle continues and repeats itself in the next generation … which inevitably affects the self-image and sense of worth of Caribbean women" (Ellis 1986: 8).

In terms of looking at solutions to enable the forging of more fulfilling and balanced male-female dynamics in relationships, it is initially important to learn how to actively listen and communicate with each other without judgement or threat to try to understand, or at the very least acknowledge, the other person's viewpoint. It is also important to find practical ways to involve and educate men beginning in preadolescence, just like girls, to be self-sufficient by knowing how to cook, clean, iron, sew, and so on. Doing so helps to prevent co-dependency issues.

There will be cases or circumstances in which more complex and deep-seated issues require third-party intervention, such as relationship counselling or attending self-help, same-sex, and or couples' groups if both parties are willing to do whatever it takes to repair the rift between them. Both parties feeling heard, valued, respected, and appreciated will go some distance towards creating the right environment for cohesion and for constructive and positive patterns to emerge in male-female relationship dynamics. Nowadays, many Caribbean-British black men share more modern views, seeing their wives as equals. Many men are great cooks and are very domesticated; with that being said it doesn't at the same time conclude that black men in relationships don't retain some notion and underlying expectation that the wife/spouse/partner should assume the lead role as the cook, carer and home-maker.

Within any male-female relationship it is always important and healthy to make quality time to go on outings and or undertake activities solely as couples to be able to reconnect and unwind. It doesn't have to involve a lot of expense. It just requires a little bit of imagination and creativity, where both parties get to enjoy one-on-one time and are able to put each other first. And most of all, to be able to learn and grow together.

The content matter discussed relating to Caribbean men and women in relationships is not static and varies to greater or lesser degrees within individual male-female relationship dynamics, combined with the changing socio-economic status pertaining to the earnings and occupations of the individual Caribbean-British male-female coupling.

The male-female relationship dynamics should also be viewed through the lens of life dating back to a different historical era and generation; although imprints and traces of behavioural patterns typically can be said to have been passed down through generations stemming from African based cultural practices, customs and habits since slavery that were transported to the Caribbean and then influenced by colonialism in the Caribbean diasporas in Western British society.

Church

All the women professed Christianity. Two of the women spoke of experiences relating to rejection by the church due to racism:

> The traditional English churches at the time were not so excepting of Caribbean families. I can recall that my husband tried to attend an Anglican church and was turned away by the priest as he said that his presence would cause the congregation to diminish. Due to this, a lot of Caribbeans began to set up their own churches. (Interviewee 4; also see Interviewee 7)

Child-minding

As discussed earlier, some of the women were forced to rely on childminders or nannies to look after their children in the absence of their mothers, extended family, and kinship networks.

I remember my parents telling stories of their earlier years living in the United Kingdom. This was one relating to a particular childminder, to whom my father had taken me prior to making his way to work. It was only the second day taking me there. He said as soon as the door opened, and I took one look at the woman before me, I began a vigorous outburst of uncontrollable bawling. In response, my dad politely excused us and took me with him. He later recalled that he simply couldn't bear to leave me under the circumstances. My facial expression on locking eyes with the childminder told a harrowing story as I was too young to express myself verbally other than in the sheer physical expression of terror! And my dad had evidently seen enough. He didn't attend work that day; he stayed at home to take care of me.

It would seem that childminders and nannies would, on occasions, come to form close bonds within the Caribbean family extended networks. Interviewees 7 and 8 formed lifelong relationships with their children's minders. It is noteworthy to point out that in the former instance, Nanny was a white Englishwoman, but she was not prejudiced against black people. On more than one occasion she took steps to address racist behaviour in protecting the black child in her care. She would go on to care for all Interviewee 7's children, all born in the United Kingdom. In the latter case, Interviewee 8 went to America for one year after the breakdown of her marriage, leaving her daughter and youngest child, who would have been approaching adolescence, with the childminder for the entire duration.

Child Mortality

Interviewees 6 and 8 suffered the loss of a child in early infancy. Interviewee 6 had already migrated to England, where she met her husband, and she had been living there for some years. She talked about finding it hard to keep warm in the house. Her baby caught a cold, fell ill, and died suddenly. Her little girl was thirteen months old. This tragedy occurred whilst living in a leasehold property between 1960 and 1967.

Interviewee 8 came to England, leaving two children back home in Jamaica. She came to England to reunite with her husband. She returned to Jamaica two years later with her third child. At the time of leaving the United Kingdom, she was in between or unsettled accommodation-wise. Her child fell ill in Jamaica. After a hurricane struck in 1951, conditions were severe, with food and medicines in short supply. Sadly, as a result, her infant died in Jamaica. (See chapter 4.)

The hurricane in Jamaica in 1951 (also documented in Fryer 1984: 373) caused a lot of damage in the region. Schools, churches, and family homes that were left standing became places of refuge as many people lost their homes, especially those made from wood. As was customary in the Caribbean, everyone pulled together in the communities to help those in greater need.

In terms of healthcare and medicines, people in the Caribbean were used to natural remedies, such as locally sourced herbs and bushes for curing various ailments. They were taught to identify and gather the right ones from a young age. Pharmaceutical medicines were costly, and most couldn't afford to buy them.

Post-war socio-economic conditions were already tough in Jamaica. Resources were limited and overstretched, and the hurricane would only have further compounded the situation. Unlike in England, where the NHS had been established in 1948, Jamaica did not have a free healthcare service in place. The NHS would serve to make the government the largest consumer of the pharmaceutical industry (Johnson, Whyman, and Wykes 1968: 90, 98). Although even in England in 1951, people were still being impacted by the war with continuing rationing in place. Many resources were limited as would have been the case in many countries at that time.

Perceptions, Lifestyle, and Cultural Habits

All of the study's women expressed having to adjust to the cold weather. Paraffin heaters were commonly used as the main heating source as there was no central heating. "People would use paraffin heaters, some used to have coal fires, but that was for the weekend. You were never lovely and warm. One night I slept in my overcoat … We used to go to the pictures [cinema] a lot. It was warm and cosy in there" (Interviewee 1).

Interviewee 6 spoke about having to dry her baby's nappies on the rack in front of the paraffin heater which blocked a lot of the heat. But that was the only way to dry the nappies. The cold was severe and caused her to reminisce about being home in Dominica in the warmth and being able to bathe in the river. Though portable paraffin heaters were commonplace, they were far from ideal. If left on overnight, they could cause nasal passages to be blocked and cause drowsiness (Bryan, Dadzie, and Scafe 1985: 130).

The majority of Caribbeans had low-paying jobs and lived in poor conditions in rundown accommodation during their early years in the United Kingdom. This made them susceptible to becoming poorly in health. This was especially true for young children during the winter months.

Many of the women said the English culture was strange because of habits the Caribbeans were unaccustomed to, such as bread being left on the pavement and fish and chips wrapped in newspaper. Washing in the kitchen sink was another strange habit to Caribbeans. The women spoke of having to use public baths and how dense the smog often was.

Caribbeans appeared to have high expectations of English life; they were taught to respect the mother country. Jamaica shared the English currency and were taught about English history in school. Caribbean colonial subjects had a deep respect for Queen and country, that had been instilled from an early age. Interviewee 8 spoke about an experience:

> When the Queen had her coronation, it was in 1952, she and husband, Prince Phillip went to Africa. Then she was told her father died and had

to come back. At the time, I was working at New Road, White Chapel, and we stood by the hospital. We begged to go out, and we promised to work back the time. They drove very, very slow, and you could see her face close up. You could run and meet up with her, it was that slow. She was beautiful, so lovely ... I also went to see King George VI lying in state. You didn't see him actually; you only saw the coffin. (Interviewee 8; chapter 4)

This sentiment was echoed in Rex and Moore by a West Indian couple who described it as the, "brainwashing of West Indians at home about Britain. They had been told about the Queen and Parliament, but no one had told them there was a colour bar" (Rex and Moore 1967: 157).

Psychologically, the women were unprepared for the reality of living in the United Kingdom. Two of the case-study women spoke of coming to Britain as, "A shock to the system." "The streets were not paved with gold," Interviewee 2 said. The truth of the matter was that life was hard and poverty widespread. The hardship, coupled with discrimination, is what bonded Caribbeans in their struggles and quests to access the housing market.

Rationing

The case-study women who arrived in 1948 and 1950 experienced rationing. Interviewee 7 is still in receipt of an original rationing book. A scanned copy can be viewed in the appendix. Rationing and building licences were wartime controls in place when the Conservatives returned to power in 1951. They had contingencies in place to begin removing these continuing controls, so by 1954, rationing and building licences were scrapped.

Caribbean Diaspora Identity

In attempting to discuss the complexity of Caribbean diaspora, identity is overlapping and ever evolving. The *Windrush* migration experience forced Caribbeans to adjust and acclimatise to their new UK environment. At the point of arrival, they came face-to-face with the harsh realities of English life. There was a steep learning curve and psychologically completely at odds with the welcoming messages and invitations extended, that had Caribbeans filled with the hope of the possibilities for abundant opportunities to be embraced in the motherland only to find out that in reality, many host residents were resentful and embittered by the immigrant presence. They viewed the immigrants as intruders—with inferior status and/or placement—of what was viewed as rightfully theirs and competition against depleted resources. This mind-set inevitably led to racial tensions and physical outbursts at a community-based level. But there was also the accompaniment of the institutional version of racism in housing and employment authorised at the government level by way of law enforcement, accompanied later by continued harassment and the policing of

Caribbean social activities and events. Despite this, Caribbean people pushed back against injustice and fought for their rights, bonding together and forming alliances.

The cultural markers associated with Caribbean society—such as music, food, social customs and traditions, and dialects—reflect the various Caribbean regions. They have been merged to form a melting pot of Caribbean identities within the United Kingdom. The Notting Hill Carnival has been an expression of this. Caribbeans have come to maintain dual identities, that of their homeland as well as of the adopted UK residence, as aptly illustrated by Homi Bhabha, cited in Murdoch:

> In large part, West Indians born in Britain actively engage with this duality, while those from the Caribbean still see the region as "home," despite the fact that they may have lived overseas for decades ... Many black British adolescents function from a position of psychological duality, whether consciously acknowledged or not ... children of migrant parents who visit the homeland often and at length feel comfortable with the language, food, music, and social structures of their ancestral space as well as their more common abode, recognising where they fit into both locales and switching gears relatively easily. (Bhabha, cited in Murdoch 2012: 51, 52)

Black African-Caribbean Identity and the Othering of Blackness

In observation of the many facets of Caribbean diaspora identity and its daily struggles living in the UK metropolis, and speaking on *The Fact of Blackness: Fantz Fanon and Visual Representation*, Alan Read explained that the purpose of the book was to stimulate discussion between Fanon's ideas and,

> on the significance of intellectual work, the politics of location, everyday traumas of social inequality, minorities and their experience of the contemporary metropolis, and artists and thinkers whose work has been concerned with the structures and technologies of representation, race and radicalism. (Read 1996: 8)

In offering an elementary interpretation of the "Othering of blackness" which steers one towards the physical characteristics of race rather than the genetics (pseudo-science), it refers to a social category, the physical appearance tied to continued forms of marginalisation and debasement in the way that specific stereotypes have been constructed to link to the visual. In turn, that affects people's emotions and perceptions that have come to impact individual and collective worldwide attitudes.

The black African-Caribbean can never be seen without the Eurocentric distorted presentation of black history assumed through the lens of savagery and slavery and implied by the colour of the black skin. It would seem that there has been a wilful omission and suppression of the black African historical legacy of identity in

Antiquity, seemingly to imply that black people didn't have any notable or thriving culture or history prior to enslavement and enforced Westernised Christianity as a civilizing tool. This is most questionable. Asa G. Hilliard speaks on facts conveyed from a 1974 UN conference in Cairo. In attendance to debate questions relating to race and civilizations in Antiquity were scholars and professors such as Cheik Anta Diop and Theophile Obenga. The outcomes documented in an official UNESCO publication are relayed by Hilliard:

> There has been generally a lack of "painstaking research" utilizing primary data in the work of most authors who have written about African people. Most often it has been the conquerors of African people or their descendants who have written about Africans, and who have done so in quite self-serving ways ... This has given the world a distorted history of African people. (Hilliard, cited in Van Sertima 1996: 90)

Hilliard goes on to discuss primary ancient literature, data, epigraphy, papyri, and so on dating back to the period of Homer in the ninth century BC in reviewing the primary research and works of Frank Snowden relating to black African cultural data. Snowden's work evidences that black Africa and black people had a prolonged affect and influence on the life and culture of Greece and Rome in Antiquity. In his examination of the language of Greece and Rome, Snowden reveals the word "Ethiopian" was used by the Greeks to denote black people of various shades in his examination of the language of Greece and Rome, made more achievable as he had lived and studied in Egypt, Greece, and Italy. Hilliard, draws reference to the substantial physical evidence unearthed by Snowdon such as:

> Many photographs of some of the primary data, including photographs of carvings, pottery, paintings, and coins. This photographic evidence is not to be disputed. As evidence it is quite unlike the undocumented assertions by traditional scholars about the history of Africans. As Snowdon indicated, it is only because racism of the present is projected by today's authors into an ancient world that did not know racism as we do, that we have become so misinformed about Africans, and therefore misinformed about history. (Ibid: 92)

Black people of Mauretania or Moor were resident in Europe in considerable numbers as a result of invasions from Africa that came to leave their traces in the records of European heraldry in several European nations. Even more intriguing is the continent of Europe, named after the African princess Europa (Van Sertima 1996: 93).

Adam Rutherford (2020), who studied genetics at University College London and is a science author and broadcaster wrote in his fascinating book, *How to Argue with a Racist,* which has given extraordinary insights into the overwhelmingly complex field of scientific modern genetics and how it can be used as a powerful tool to disempower racists against the abuse of pseudo-science or flawed outdated theories and or assumptions to justify racism. Rutherford draws reference to the Kuba tribe people in what is now known as the Democratic Republic of Congo in central Africa. Formerly within this location was the Kuba Kingdom ruled by King Shyaam, who unified the local tribes to what would become an organised and co-ordinated city state. (Rutherford, 2020: 54) Rutherford conveys that the Kuba Kingdom was an advanced state at that time compared to many African societies of the era, predating Belgium colonisation:

> The Kuba Kingdom shared characteristics of modern political systems, a capital, an oral constitution, a tiered legal system, trial by jury, taxation and a police force. Following colonisation, the kingdom was weakened, but still exists within the Democratic Republic of Congo, and many people identify as Kuba. (Rutherford, 2020: 54)

It has been suggested by Fryer, that England within the era of the sixteenth and seventeenth centuries felt threatened by the knowledge of darker skinned peoples due to the fact that England had been more isolated than their Spanish and Portuguese European counterparts. Who had been subsequently invaded and conquered by darker skinned races who possessed a higher structure of civilisation than themselves:

> The insular English, whose historical experience had been more limited, found sudden contact with black Africans deeply disturbing. It was a severe cultural shock for them: 'one of the fairest skinned nations suddenly came face to face with one of the darkest people on earth'. Not merely did the Wolofs and Mandings of Senegambia fail to fit the English ideal; they 'seemed the very picture of perverse negation. (Fryer, 1984: 135)

However, before this shocking confrontation on foreign territory, English people had had knowledge of black people. In fact, there has been a black presence on British soil albeit very isolated and scattered, even before the English (Fryer, 1984: 1). Furthermore, in support of an African presence in early England, Edward Scobie cited in Van Sertima (1996) talks of work carried out by Dr Leslie Hotson, a renowned Shakespearean scholar who has carried out extensive research on the origins of the Dark Lady Love[3] of Shakespeare's sonnets:

In the old age black was not counted fair,

Or if it were, it bore not beauty's name;

---

[3] Lucy Negro: Shakespeare's Dark Lady love was a famous courtesan. African women were seen as highly desirable sex symbols in Europe from the fifteenth and sixteenth centuries onwards. (Van Sertima, 1996: 207-208).

But now is black beauty's successive heir.

If her hairs be wires, black wires grow on her head.

I have seen roses damask'd red and white,

But no such roses see I in her cheeks.

(Van Sertima, 1996: 207-208)

These sonnets were written around 1597 and 1598. Coupled with this, the point is made that during this time period in London there was a considerable African presence and large numbers of African women also lived in the location of Clerkenwell. Fryer also makes mention to the existence of Shakespeare's Dark Lady love. (Fryer, 1984: 9).

Rutherford further reveals that in 2016, the discovery of the DNA of what he describes as an ancient Briton, called 'Cheddar Man' Rutherford, (2020: 36). The genetical evidence dated his existence way before:

> The Picts, Romans, Vikings, Angles or Saxons ... Cheddar Man is predicted to have had dark or dark to black skin, blue/green eyes and dark brown possibly black ... tightly curled hair. The DNA evidence had shown that he lacked pigmentation alleles that are associated with light skin ... When these pictures hit the news, racists all around the world lost their collective marbles with splenetic fury. Although as Rutherford exclaims ... that there were dark-skinned people in Europe 10,000 years ago is not at all controversial... (Rutherford, 2020: 36)

Despite the continued historical and political generational trauma of racism, displacement, exclusion, oppression, exploitation and drain of regional colonial resources, black people in Africa, the Caribbean, and throughout the Western metropolitan regions continue to rebel, resist, endure, and rise up against all the odds and throughout the ages, giving credence to black people's, "Staying Power", as so accurately put by Peter Fryer (1984). But by the same token, no matter how Christianised, civilized, or educated, black people remain under the racialized look as other.

The elements of racist discourse that Stuart Hall conveys regarding Fanon's *Black Skin, White Masks* is part of, as Hall highlights, a series of, "unfinished dialogues", in drawing on French psychoanalyst and psychiatrist Jacques Lacan's ontological (concerning the nature of being) discourse which inspired Fanon's opposing stance that states,

> The real "Other" for the white man is and will continue to be the black man … Ontology does not permit us to understand the being of the black man. For not only must the black man be black; he must be black in relation to the white man. (Hall, cited in Read 1996: 26, 27)

It would seem that with the continual advancement of modern scientific technology it's certainly time to finally start focusing on our commonalities rather than our differences as human beings as Rutherford enlightens us that there is no such thing as a pure or distinct race and the origins of *Homo sapiens* commenced some 70,000 years ago in the authentic motherland, Africa. (Rutherford, 2020: 28)

Black British-Caribbean Identity: A Personal Viewpoint

From a personal perspective, as a female child of Caribbean parents, growing up I never saw myself as being British. I never felt that sense of belonging, pride, patriotism, or identity with my country of birth. I always felt being black got in the way of these sentiments. The political structuring of UK society chose self-classification of individual cultural identity and ethnicity status along racially constructed lines—such as black or black British, Caribbean; African; or other black background—to reveal or determine direct ancestral roots. This is required in completing official documentation in employment, medical, educational, or social aspects of daily living. Regardless of being born British, you're still required, or at least strongly encouraged, to state your parents' region of birth. This is a general point of reference in most formal and informal information exchanges.

In fact, I felt more in tune with my Britishness when travelling away from the United Kingdom than when residing here. Growing up as an impressionable child living in North London, the education I was receiving in school at the time fuelled a sense of marginality as the omission of self in the history being taught; British history didn't include black people. And on TV, there was only a mere sprinkling of black figures. There were no black people in advertisements on TV either. You would even see programmes such as *The Black and White Minstrel Show* blatantly on the screen (white people in blackface mimicking black people). I never understood how this was accepted or seen as okay.

In the earlier days, my parents, two younger brothers, and I lived in South Tottenham, in a tight-knit Caribbean community. On our street we were a close neighbourhood of black Jamaican families that were in and out of each other's houses; there was a strong sense of Caribbean identity. There was many a house party, domino-playing by the men, and the nostalgia of back home amongst our Jamaican kinfolk. As a little girl, I remember the blue spot music centre with radio that my mother spoke about in her interview (Interviewee 1), taking pride of place in the living room. I especially remember it pounding out good vibrations and giving way to a strong sense of Caribbean pride and belonging as our story intertwined in beautiful Caribbean music that was so irresistibly compelling that you had to move to the beat! Born out of Jamaican *'Rastafarian'* culture, reggae music would come to hold an international stage as an artistic expression of resistance; the struggle for liberation and Pan-African solidarity. Reggae music embodied the traditions of *"militant resistance to racism,"* tied to the *"traditions of Garveyism".* (Lewis and Bryan 1991) Owing to the prominent vocalist Bob Marley; the heart of the global black masses. Along with many other conscious musicians worldwide who rejected apartheid (1948–1994) and revealed: *"those African leaders who co-operated with apartheid against the oppressed majority in South Africa and Namibia".* (Lewis and Bryan 1991: 182) The music ranged from reggae to ska, calypso, or soca, and then lover's rock in my teenage years and twenties. Rhythm and blues and soul music, too, as we were influenced by black American popular culture, and especially because we had extended family and kinship ties over there.

Food was always a powerful connector to the culture. My mother loved to cook, and she was very good at it. The traditional Saturday soups, such as beef soup and red peas soup, were the favourites. But there were others, such as fish tea soup and mannish water. Then we have the Sunday roast dinner of chicken, pork (my father loved pork), beef, or a lamb joint. Or maybe some stewed boiler chicken or chicken fried in breadcrumbs—whatever they could afford that week—with rice and peas, roast potatoes, a potato and cheese bake, or macaroni and cheese, and homemade coleslaw. With refreshments such as carrot juice, pineapple punch, or guinness punch; (that we weren't allowed to drink on account of the alcohol until we were older, unless you took a sneaky sip without being caught). And sorrel during the holiday festive season. Lastly, the feast would be rounded off with jelly and ice cream or a homemade fruit cocktail trifle for dessert. Or something more indulgent if Mother was in the mood to bake a cake or when we had guests over, namely relatives or friends. My brother's and I loved to use our little fingers to scoop up and devour the yummiest leftover cake mixture until the bowl was clean. Sunday dinner was my favourite dinner of the week.

This doesn't begin to cover Mother's culinary skills and the variety of Caribbean dishes that she'd prepare in the kitchen. Later, she did a series of twenty-five recorded interviews with a lady from the British Library (Migration Archive Stories), talking about Caribbean food and the catering industry, as well as her childhood experiences growing up in Jamaica. We didn't have much; my parents worked hard. They couldn't afford fancy presents at Christmastime, just the essentials, such as socks and underwear. But we were always well fed. They made sure of that.

After worshipping further afield—mainly at the Seventh Day Adventist Church, the denomination my mother grew up in, in Jamaica—over time, my mother and other Caribbean women living on our street and neighbouring roads, came to make their presence felt in the pews of the Anglican Church across the road from our house.

Their action stimulated it to become more racially inclusive as we were obviously not going away.

By the time I got into my adolescent years, we moved to mid-Tottenham, and the rose-tinted glasses of being sheltered within the family nest and the early childhood street full of innocence and fun and frolics was gone. My parents could no longer shield me. I had to go out into the big bad world and face the reality of racism that was apparent in Tottenham as in other areas with a dense Caribbean presence. The backdrop of living within a black community plagued by racial tensions and deep-seated scepticism towards the police stemming from their heavy-handed dealings and approach towards black people, and who seemed determined to torment and tarnish the image of the upcoming British-born next generation of black youth.

This heightened our sense of community solidarity and commitment to self-empowerment and improvement. We knew our parents' history of struggles since their arrivals in the United Kingdom. And the oppressive treatment that led black people to resistance and to devise self-help measures and strategies in housing, in education, in striving for better occupations, and in black people's entitlement to equal rights and black self-dignity as human beings in a system seeking to use force, brutality, and control, rendering black people with no choice other than to stand up for their rights.

A poignant memory of this is the Broadwater Farm riots of 6 October 1985. The situation had been gaining momentum since an incident took place about a week or so earlier in Brixton. The police shot Dorothy "Cherry" Groce twice in September 1985, paralysing her and confining her to a wheelchair for the rest of her life. This sparked riots in Brixton.

Then came the death of Cynthia Jarrett at the hands of the police—in particular DC Randall—on 5 October 1985. The police illegally entered Mrs Jarrett's home after detaining her son, Floyd Jarrett, after a routine stop and search procedure carried out by the police under the legislated 'sus' laws once they have 'reasonable grounds for suspicion' (Benyon, 1986: 15). The sus laws were brought into action by utilising section 4 of the Vagrancy Act, 1824; allowing the police to be able to arrest and detain a person who appeared to be loitering, acting suspiciously or with an intent to commit an unlawful deed. Being that there didn't need to be firm evidence of any kind to support the police suspicions, meant that the police had the power to stop, search and arrest for the flimsiest of reasons. As such, it has often been claimed that the police regularly exploited these powers (Benyon, 1986: 14). In the case of Floyd Jarrett his BMW car tax disc was out of date. To which he explained that he had only just returned from Jamaica as part of a youth exchange trip. The police proceeded to search his car for stolen or prohibited items; but Mr Jarrett had his pregnant girlfriend in the passenger seat, started to become concerned about her welfare and asked if he could be allowed to continue his journey. From there onwards the situation would take a downhill spiral and turned into a verbal exchange. The police accused Mr Jarrett of assaulting an officer, which was firmly denied by Mr Jarrett and his girlfriend and on suspicion of car theft, both of which he was later acquitted. Floyd Jarrett was a 23-year-old Haringey black community resident, who also worked at the Broadwater Farm Youth Association (Benyon, 1986: 9). While he was detained at the station, the police confiscated his house keys and entered the property without warning to search for incriminating evidence, leading to the death of his mother Mrs Cynthia Jarrett and also witnessed by Floyd's sister Patricia Jarrett. The Jarrett Family accused the police of assault and lack of due diligence in an urgency to request an ambulance, (Benyon, 1986: 9, 10; The Institute of Race Relations 1987: 25, 85; People's Account 1985, London Community Video Archive [LCVA]: 2018).

The protest rally from Broadwater Farm was meant to be a peaceful demonstration condemning the brutality of the police in light of the recent shooting, and the subsequent death after a police raid; both amounting to needless tragedies involving two innocent women. But the situation took a sour turn when the police came in full force, dressed in riot gear, and blocked the exits to prevent people from leaving the Broadwater Farm estate. This incited further anger in an already sensitive situation in which black people were exercising their freedom of speech. This led to the violent backlash in which the white officer PC Blakelock lost his life, adding to the recent death count. (People's Account, LCVA, 2018).

I remember the chaos of that evening. I was eighteen years old, the same age my mother was when she came to the United Kingdom. Our house was roughly within five to ten minutes walking distance from the scene. Helicopter activity could be heard from above, and echoing noises of disruption in the air when you approached the front door and stood in the front garden. But the true gravity of what happened was only fully realised the following day. None of the police officers involved were charged by the Police Complaints Authority, but following an independent inquiry review headed by Lord Gifford QC, concluded that:

> There were sufficient grounds to support charges against the officers for the following disciplinary offences: abuse of authority, discreditable conduct, racially discriminatory behaviour, neglect of duty, and falsehood and prevarication. The inquiry concluded that the 'Police Complaints Authority failed lamentably in its investigation ... to satisfy a large section of the public, including ourselves, of its independence and impartiality' and that the 'case of Mrs Jarrett's death ... calls into question whether members of the Authority who were party to the decision should continue to hold their responsible public office'... *Broadwater Farm Inquiry,* (The Institute of Race Relations, 1987: 84, 85).

In the eyes of the black community the police were deemed to be institutionally racist following the Broadwater Farm Inquiry that took place in 1986.

The tabloid press was also shown to be complacent in giving the full facts linked to the escalating chain of horrifying occurrences. It would seem the newspapers were intent on showing black youth and even the black Tottenham Labour Party constituent MP Bernie Grant, who publicly condemned the police actions, in a negative light to suit the police narrative (People's Account, LCVA: 2018). By the time of the 1985 riots, the press had concocted an image of black activism and outside agitation linked to Moscow and Libya and anchoring it to the violence.

The press, such as *The Times* and the *Daily Express* labelled Bernie Grant, as well as a number of other black and white local Labour Party constituent members as propagators of race hate. Douglas Hurd, Conservative former secretary of state for Northern Ireland, who held office during the governments of Margaret Thatcher and John Major (1979–1997), purported that Bernie Grant and others to be the, "high priests of race hate" (Solomos 1993: 166).

The *Daily Express* reported following the death of PC Blakelock on Broadwater Farm,

> The thugs who murdered policeman Keith Blakelock in the Tottenham riots acted on the orders of crazed left-wing extremists. Street-fighting experts trained in Moscow and Libya … a hand-picked death squad … sent into North London hell-bent on bloodshed. They include men and women from Commonwealth countries like Jamaica, Barbados and Nigeria, who have been trained in Russia and Libya in street revolutionary tactics. (Benyon, 1986: 10; Solomos, 1993: 167).

This diversion of discursive positioning sought to deflect the cause of the riots away from the real issue of racism, as with the 1958 Notting Hill Riots, and the social aspects tied to inner-city black communities. But instead, it distorted the situation and sent racial hatred spiralling as the effects of the extreme left and black activists. As pointed out by Solomos, then columnist Ronald Butt, who worked for *The Times* and other newspapers, writing about racial issues between 1980, 1981, and 1985, Solomos highlights that "Race had become a new weapon in the class war" (Solomos 1993: 166). Jones's (1994) assessment of law and order and political ideas, and in encompassing a cultural theoretical framework is that it rests on human's personal views and lived experiences, but also humans' propensity towards self-interest and personal gain. Showing various philosopher's perspectives; Machiavelli who theorised that:

> It may be said of men in general that they are ungrateful, voluble dissemblers, anxious to avoid danger and covetous of gain. (Jones, 1994: 355) Marx held the view that, *'environment determines consciousness'* and it was discordance of the capitalist economic system which has served to exacerbate man's flaws. (Ibid: 355)

Jones relays that Rosseau believed that, *'man is naturally good and only by institutions is he made bad'.* (Ibid:355) There were others who swayed towards an increasingly cynical view, such as Thomas Hobbes, who's political philosophy held a more pessimistic stance that in order to keep the likelihood of chaos and anarchy at bay it was necessary to have in place the authority of an *'all powerful state'* as an institution of force. Returning to Marx; Jones (1994) specifies how Marx saw the only solution to tackling deviance was by bringing about significant changes with a more egalitarian society with fairness and justice at its core. Rather than a society based on the interests of the capitalist ruling class. In looking at these ideas and how it relates to Conservative verses Labour and Liberal Democrat governments. Jones states that Conservatives lean towards a rigid and a glass half empty pessimism. *'Respect for the rule of laws is the basis of free and civilised society' - 1979 manifesto.* (Jones, 1994: 356) Whereas Labour and the Liberal Democrats held a glass half full optimism; such as a belief that crime is closely associated with social deprivation; poverty, poor housing, and unemployment, which was thought could be successfully addressed and reduced by way of social policy. (Ibid: 356)

One of the beliefs of right-wing analysis of the Thatcher government was that:

> Excessive immigration of alien peoples had created tensions and further weakened cultural restraints against lawless behaviour. It was also voiced by Margaret Thatcher that trade unions, aided by extremist left-wing groups and tacitly by the Labour Party, have increasingly ignored the law and used violence and intimidation – 'the rule of the mob' to achieve their industrial and political objections. (Jones, 1994: 362-363)

Whereas left-wing analysis relating to crime placed the problem largely to the economic system, rejecting the right-wing approach as:

> A mere rationalisation of ruling-class interests; many 'values' which workers are enjoined to embrace are those which favour not them but the ruling middle class. (Ibid: 363)

Jones further draws out that the left-wing school of thought felt that,

> The law protects the privileges of the rich through prosecuting and punishing 'working-class crime' such as robbery and vandalism with much greater energy than 'middle-class crime', e.g., fraud and expenses fiddling. For example, in 1981 the state lost £4 million a week through social security frauds and made 576 prosecutions, yet lost £80 million a week through tax evasion and made only two prosecutions per week. Moreover, since 1979 the Conservative government has taken on 1,000 social security investigators yet has actually reduced the size of the tax inspectorate. (Jones, 1994: 363)

Essentially as discussed earlier the racial tensions that erupted during the '80s, would become a weapon for undermining Labour party politics and particular MPs who spoke transparently about the need to combat racial injustice within Black

Minority Ethnic (BME) communities in Britain. This tactic could be claimed to have worked in favour of Conservative party politics and in helping to sway public opinion towards maintaining the political status quo.

✳✳✳✳ ✳✳✳✳ ✳✳✳✳ ✳✳✳✳

In continuing to ponder on the black British-Caribbean identity from a personal perspective, my darker complexion and my very shrinkable, tight-curled, kinky afro hair served as a very real deterrent for participating in school curriculum-based swimming lessons. Even with the swimming cap secured, water always seeped in. Plus, the stylish braiding of hair wasn't one of my mother's skills, though she tried her best. (I would later teach myself.) Self-image is always an important feature, especially during the secondary school years. And I was no exception.

Being black is an inescapable difference, the visual "othering" that makes it impossible to just be. Then there was always the awareness and schooling from my parents and Caribbean elders that as a black person, you had to be better and work harder to succeed. There was always the visual reminder via the media and television of feeling different and that you needed to try to meet the Eurocentric standard of beauty, such as feeling the need to straighten our hair by pressing or relaxing of black women's hair. After all, hair is as much an identifier as race, as informed by Stuart Hall, who concurs that,

> through a process of displacement, along the chain of equivalences; hair, skin, bone, genitals … come to symbolise … black skin—big penis— small brain—poor and backward—it's all in the genes—end the poverty programme—send them home! … because their arrangement within a discursive chain enables physiological signs to function as signifiers to stand for and be "read" further up the chain; socially, psychically, cognitively, politically, culturally, civilisationally. (Hall, cited in Read 1996: 20, 21, 24)

An example of this that made me shudder at the extent of the teddy boys' premeditated actions. Relating back to my parents' and the case-study women's times of arrival in the United Kingdom, speaking on black women's realities of daily living as relayed by Bryan, Dadzie, and Scafe:

> In those days, there was a lot of racism with teddy boys … one day I was going to work and it was very foggy. I knew these chaps behind me were white. Then one of them came up alongside me and felt my hair. My hair was straightened at the time, and he said, "This one's hair feels white, so leave her alone." Then one of the others shouted, "There's a nigger, over there." Whoever it was, she really got some kicks—you could hear her screaming. But things like this helped us to band together. We were all West Indians! (Bryan, Dadzie, and Scafe 1985: 133)

The problem is not in the act of straightening our hair; it's a legitimate choice if that's what we desire to do. It's okay. But black women shouldn't feel compelled to straighten their hair in order to fit in or to be accepted. I have grown into the black women that I am today learning from and appreciating black women's powerful presence as being naturally beautiful, resilient, unique, versatile, frequently having to multitask, and possessing the right to express herself in whatever way she chooses and that allows her to feel comfortable from within. It's all about self-love and self-expression.

However, growing up and seeing some white people's conflicting attitudes, the negative media, and lack of a positive black history being taught in school left their marks on my psyche from an early age. In my younger-day mentality, everything was simple. Why couldn't we just all get along? How comes we have various types of flowers, plants and animals on the planet, and it's okay? Why is it that differences in skin colour and other differences in people cause so much ridicule, pain, sadness, and suffering, yet human beings are meant to be the most intelligent of all the life forms? These feelings of antagonism culminated in a deep sense of melancholy seclusion or of being unaccepted in my birth country that also led to insecurities and not feeling beautiful, no matter how much my mother told me otherwise. Or that I was enough as a black woman.

Indeed, it's taken me some time to find that unconditional love of self and to be comfortable in my own skin. Although apart from my mother, who connected with how I felt, it was a feeling that was suppressed. Deep down was a sense of lack, frustration, resentment, and inadequacy. I couldn't explain to myself, let alone to anyone else. Only now laying bare, during the epiphany of the documentary unravelling, stirred up emotions that has compelled me to free the soul and speak my truth as a first-generation British-born Caribbean descendant. There was the sentiment that the black woman got a raw deal, not just as a minority ethnic group, but generally living in a patriarchal society.

As a result, I was content to discard my Britishness, preferring to embrace my African-Caribbean-ness to the fullness. Growing up, ours was a typical Caribbean family, re-enacting and cherishing the Caribbean traditions of my Jamaican parents.

My first taste of Jamaica came with a family holiday when I was six years old. I remember my introduction to chicken foot soup, the intense heat, travelling on the train from Kingston to the northern coast, Montego Bay, to visit my grandparents on my father's side. There I met my affectionate grandmother, whom I was named after. I loved the fireflies at night. I fantasised that they were fairies at the time. I remember the suddenness of the rain showers that dried up so fast you would never believe they happened.

There was the beautifully mesmerising turquoise sea—beach, where I learnt that, astonishingly to me, my mother couldn't swim—only my father could. I fell in love with Jamaica. Even so, I wasn't to return until some thirty years later. I was born in England, but Jamaica will always be my ancestral home. There will always be that dual connection. Jamaica is in my blood, as is Africa.

Women's Comparative Analysis Chart

The following chart was designed to make it easier to identify, compare, and examine migration/Windrush women's collective experiences or identify differences, thereby providing quantitative and qualitative insights. Sections where information has been omitted from the chart means that I was not privy to that information so was unable to provide a definitive answer.

Caribbean Women's Migration: Windrush Comparative Analysis Chart

	Interviewee 1	Interviewee 2	Interviewee 3	Interviewee 4	Interviewee 5	Interviewee 6	Interviewee 7	Interviewee 8
Country of Birth	Jamaica	Jamaica	Jamaica	Jamaica	Guyana	Dominica	Jamaica	Jamaica
Year of Arrival	1955	1961	1962	1961	1958	1957	1950	1948
Age	77	73	68	84	77	83	85	85
Mode of Travel	Ship	Ship	Plane	Plane	Ship	Ship	Ship	Ship
Earliest Arrival	3rd	7th (Nov)	8th	6th (May)	5th	4th	2nd	1st
Total Years in UK to 2014: Approximate Figures	59	53	52	53	56	57	64	66
Experienced Rationing	No	No	No	No	No	No	Yes (In receipt of a Ration Book)	Yes
Involved in Pardner Savings Scheme	Yes	No	Yes	Yes	Yes	Yes	Yes	Yes
Bought Home in UK	Yes	Yes	Yes	Yes	Yes	Yes	Yes	Yes
Currently Live in Owned Property in UK	Yes	Yes	No	Yes	Yes	Yes	No	Yes
Own Property in Caribbean	No		Yes	No		No	Yes	No

	1	2	3	4	5	6	7	8
Lived in the Same Private Rental Property in Early Days as Another Interviewee	Yes: Wray Crescent, Hornsey, N8; Jamaican landlady between 1956 and 1957				Yes: Wray Crescent, Hornsey, N8; Jamaican landlady in 1960			
Private Rental Accommodation: Renter Nationality	Jewish and Caribbean	Caribbean	Caribbean	Jewish and Caribbean	Jewish and Caribbean	Jewish and Caribbean	English and Canadian, Caribbean, Polish	English
Had to Adjust to Climate—Complained of the Cold	Yes	Yes	Yes	Yes	Yes	Yes	Yes	Yes
Came to UK to Work and Make a Better Life	Yes	Yes	Came to join Father and Stepmother.	Yes	Yes	Yes	Yes	Yes
Experienced Overt Racism	Yes	Yes	No	Yes	Yes	Yes	Yes	Yes
Found Difficulty Maintaining Private Rented Accommodation once Started Having Children	Not Applicable; did not have children during early years.	Yes	No	Yes	Yes	Yes	Yes	Yes
Early Occupations	Worked in the 'rag trade'	Smith's Crisps Factory	Worked in admin in the rag trade	Worked in a post office canteen	Worked in a sweets factory	Worked for a firm making costume jewellery	Worked in the 'rag trade'	Worked in the rag trade

Described Wages as Being Cheap	Yes	Yes	Yes	Yes	Yes	Yes	Yes	Yes
Experienced Discrimination at Work	Yes		Yes		Yes		No	
Duration Spent in Last Owned Property/Address	1982–present = 32 years	1969–present = 45 years	1973–2010 = 37 years	1987–present = 27 years	1975–present = 39 years	1969–present = 45 years	1958–1989 = 41 years; 1989–2009 = 20 years	1969–present = 45 years
Religion/	C of E	C of E	C of E	Seven Day Adventist	Catholic	Catholic	Brethren	Catholic
Denomination	Christian	Christian	Christian	Christian	Christian	Christian	Christian	Christian
Received Education/ Schooling in the UK	No	No	Yes	No	No	No	No	No
Experienced Exclusion from the Church			No	Yes			Yes	Mentioned that church's congregation was practically non-existent when first arrived.
Already Had Children in the Caribbean before Coming to the UK	No	Yes	No	Yes	No	Yes	No	Yes

Had Children Who Died in Early Infancy in the Caribbean or in the UK	No	No	No	No	No	Yes	No	Yes
Experienced Problems with Caribbean Landlords	Yes	Yes		Yes	Yes			
Described Life as Hard When First Arrived	Yes	Yes	Not so much	Got hard once started having children; couldn't get places to rent.	Yes	Yes		Yes
Sent for Children/ Spouses in the Caribbean	No	Yes	Not applicable	Yes	No	Yes	No	Yes
Experienced Poor/ Overcrowded Conditions in Private Rental, Lacked Basic Amenities	Yes	Yes	Not so much	Yes	Yes	Yes	Yes	Yes

Figure 12: Rationing in Britain during WWII, 1942

This image shows a tray containing the ration book for a Mr Norman Franklin and his weekly rations of sugar, tea, margarine, 'national butter', lard, eggs, bacon and cheese, circa 1942.

Source: Imperial War Museums, Photo by Ministry of Information photo division photographer, IWM via Getty Images.

Ration books, which were in effect during and after WWII, when there were food shortages in Britain. This continued until 1954. Ration books were later supplied for clothing and furniture (MoDA, Museum of Domestic Design & Architecture, Middlesex University: 2014). As mentioned, Clothing ration books were also in circulation; clothes were recycled and reused. Giving an indication of the times and hardships faced by the general population following the war and the scarcity of resources (Royal Museums Greenwich: 2014).

CHAPTER 6

Conclusion

This discourse documents the housing history and intimate lives of women who travelled to Britain as part of a unique colonial period of mass migration by Caribbean men, women, and children commonly referred to as the *Windrush* era.

Migration has been a common occurrence throughout the ages by various ethnic groups. This topic flags issues relevant to current immigration anxieties and complexities and raise concerns for ongoing discussion and analysis today. They include matters such as competing for limited or dwindling resources. The legitimacy of entitlement perceived by the host societies over the new arrivals when it comes to accessing jobs, housing, and healthcare continue to be of relevance and stir political debate in the United Kingdom.

However, the Caribbean people at the time of *Windrush* migration and before shared a familiar bond tied to Britain's colonial governance. Active in the British West Indian Islands uniquely linked them to queen and country as colonial subjects in a way that is different from modern immigrant societies coming to the United Kingdom.

The British West Indian's stratified systems of class-based societies, education, worship, currency, and even sports; most popularly for example, games such as cricket were influenced and transferred according to the British model. The Caribbean psyche was geared to obtaining the British standard. Caribbean girls and boys sang the British national anthem in their schools. These British legacies were handed down since slavery (Stone, cited in Lewis and Bryan 1991: 243–4). In order to contextualize the extent of the psychological conditioning of the masses in Caribbean society, from childhood, I will share my mother's innocent, youthful story. It relates to the death of King George VI, on February 6, 1952. Prior to hearing the news, my mother was sent on an errand to the local store; where a radio announcement was aired. Upon hearing this revelation, my mother suddenly burst into tears and ran home crying, forgetting about what she was sent to buy. On her return, her elder sister anxiously asked what was the matter? To which my mother exclaimed, "King George is dead!". She was 14 years old, at the time; living in Jamaica, approximately 4,561 miles from England, which amounts to more or less a ten-hour plane flight. Such was the far-reaching impact of British colonialism in its Caribbean territories. The women in this case study describe Britain as the mother country, and through their expressions and body language, reveal a patriotic sense of pride in appropriating the title of British colonial subject to a colonial motherland which typically did not reciprocate the same sentiment.

In analysis, Caribbeans went to extreme lengths to travel great distances, initially by ship, which caused women, men, and children in later years to be at sea for weeks at a time. Indeed, the case-study women spoke of instances when large numbers of the passengers fell ill. This determination to make a better life could be likened to that of a visionary or even an entrepreneurial drive (Bell, cited in Ellis 1986: 47), possibly tied in with a romanticised image of England. Caribbean men and women seemed to have made very conscious and committed decisions against the odds to travel to the United Kingdom with the firm belief that they could derive a job, a home, further training/education, and generally have better survival prospects.

Although undoubtedly challenging in terms of accessing housing and becoming property owners, living in Britain afforded Caribbeans a unique opportunity as property was cheap, although wages were also minimal. Remaining focused and through pardner schemes, many Caribbeans were able to get a foothold on the property ladder and achieve their home owning aspirations. This aspiration is not financially attainable to many British-born Caribbean descendants with the same homeownership desires living in the United Kingdom today.

In fact, in 2022, in England we've returned to the period prior to the Housing Act of 1919, as shown earlier in the Office for National Statistics (ONS) Census Figure 5 image: Home ownership and renting from 1918-2011. Where it maps the changes over the period (1918-2011) commencing when private rental was the dominant form of tenancy for the British household. Moving on from the housing depletion of the inter-war period; after a much-needed government emphasis on house building; and particularly social housing properties, which are homes rented from a local authority or housing association. Home ownership started to become increasingly popular from 1939 onwards and accelerated with the Thatcher government's implementation of the Right to Buy initiative stemming from the 1980s, onwards, up until 2001, where homeownership acquisition peaked. Social housing occupancy was overtaken by a surge in home ownership during the early millennium due to the Right to Buy scheme, and gradually we have witnessed a shift back towards private rental that accelerated from 2011. This was inevitable as affordable social housing was not being built to replace the social housing being sold in the private market. Although, as documented by Vicky Spratt (2022), housing journalist and activist; this rise and fall in social housing availability leading to this so-called housing 'crisis' follows a traceable series of unfolding events that has been in the making for the last three decades:

> This was as predictable as it was avoidable. The housing crisis is made up of a series if distinct but related emergencies: the instability of the private rented sector; rising street and hidden homelessness; unaffordable housing enabled by our country's economic reliance on the housing market; the hoarding of property wealth; and deliberate undoing of our welfare safety net and the intentional but artificial inflation of our housing market in the past thirty years. All of these have resulted in the endemic inequality that has become the status quo in Britain. (Spratt, 2022: 12)

For comparative purposes it was felt important to ponder on the deepening predicament of housing in twenty first century Britain. Housing provision has been retarded to the point of retrograde; familiar to the start of the Windrush era relating to this discourse. Further showing the qualitative importance, empowerment and rewards of collective self-help initiatives, (such as the pardner schemes) taken by Caribbeans in dire circumstances that were to provide a unique opportunity and solution for many Caribbean migrants in Britain and would subsequently serve as a springboard to meeting the Caribbean women's home ownership aspirations during the post WWII regenerative period.

The primary case-study research and literature enquiry served to illuminate and confirm women's marginalised positions at the time of the post-war *Windrush* era. The case studies show that despite this, women took the initiative in working and shaping their destinies. They were not passive bystanders, relying solely on men to provide for them. Nevertheless, women's frail positioning would have a significant bearing on the lack of literature on black women of the Caribbean diaspora living in the United Kingdom.

Windrush women, I thank you and salute you for your strength and determination in overcoming adversity and for imparting your inspirational testimonies introduced through your housing history.

As a testament to Caribbean women's contributions, good works, and endurance, as well as being trailblazers and inspiration for each new generation of black women living in the United Kingdom, tribute is paid to an early champion of black women's achievements in history. In remembrance of Mrs Mary Seacole, aka Mary Jane Grant. Born in 1805 in Kingston, Jamaica, a Colonial British subject, she grew up within slave society. She was a woman of many skills and talents. She was a gifted healer, having followed in the footsteps of her mother, who in the words of Fryer (1984: 246) was, "a competent practitioner of Jamaican medicine." Mary Seacole was widely travelled.

Although mostly remembered for her humanitarian, nursing, and medical care provided to soldiers in the British Army whilst fighting in the Crimean War from

1853–1856, This brave, forthright, jovial, resourceful, and resilient coloured woman became a popular figure of her time with her first book published by James Blackwood in July 1857. Over time, her life story faded into obscurity, resurfacing only with a splendid second edition of her autobiography by Alexander and Dewjee in July 1999. Mary Jane Seacole is often fondly referred to by Caribbeans as the black Florence Nightingale. She died 14 May 1881 in England.

Punch published a poem in February 1856 in honour of her medical care and kindly deposition, which was a great source of upliftment and healing for wounded British soldiers in the war at that time (Alexander and Dewjee 1999: 9, 30, 37).

A Stir for Seacole

Dame Seacole was a kindly old soul,

And a kindly old soul was she,

You might call for your pot, you might

call for your pipe,

In her tent on "the Col" so free …

That berry-brown face, with a kind heart's trace

Impressed in each wrinkle sly,

Was a sight to behold, through the snow-clouds

rolled Across that iron sky …

The sick and sorry can tell the story

Of her nursing and dosing deeds,

Regimental M.D. never worked as she

In helping sick men's needs …

—Be the right man in the right place who can—

The right woman was Dame Seacole!

Punch 1856, cited in Alexander and Dewjee 1999: 235, 236

APPENDICES

Appendix One

Interviewee 7's original ration book. (1953–1954)

Source: Dorrel Green-Briggs, Photo by Dorrel Green-Briggs.

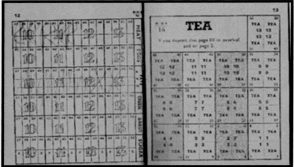

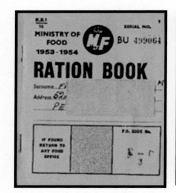
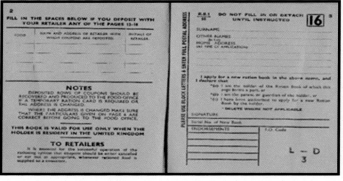

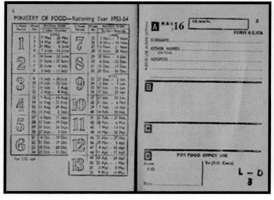
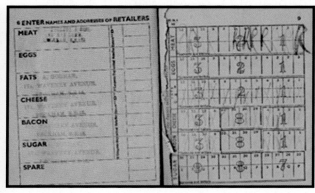

Appendix Two

Family Archive Photographs: (Interviewee 1)

My mother (Bride) and her sisters on wedding day, June 1958

My parents were wed at Tottenham Baptist Church, London N17 in June 1958. Photo taken (below) at wedding reception, held at 14 West bank, London N16.

Appendix Three

Mother's British passport, (Interviewee 1) showing her occupation as a dressmaker in Jamaica, prior to immigrating to the United Kingdom.

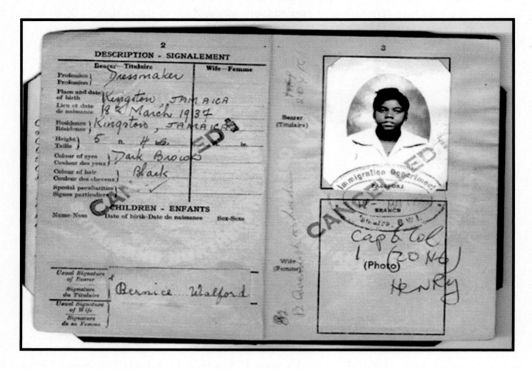

My mother's passport identifies her immigration status as being a Citizen of the United Kingdom and Colonies - (CUKC).

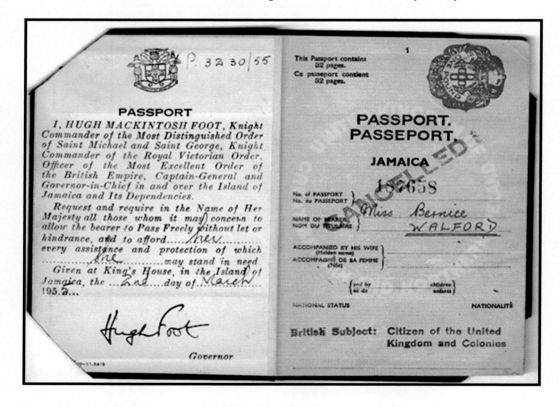

ABOUT THE AUTHOR

I grew up in south Tottenham, North east London. The only daughter, and eldest of three children of Jamaican born parents; Bertram Ranfurly Green and Bernice Millicent Green. My parents came to England during the 1950s Windrush era. Born in May 1967, my brothers and I fall into the category of first (Windrush) generation, UK born British citizens of Caribbean decent. Our family was situated in an ethnic cluster of Caribbean families to form our own small community amongst the concentrated Jewish community region in South Tottenham.

On the street of my childhood home stood the inviting presence of St. Bartholomew's Anglican church. More or less opposite our terraced house. It was inevitable that my mother would eventually become a diligent and active member, mainly because of the close proximity to our home. My mother grew up as a Seventh day Adventist in Jamaica, whilst my father's Christian roots stemmed from the Baptist denomination. The church was a fundamental part of my parent's life, but especially for my mother. Her faith supported and comforted her throughout the storms of life and all its challenges. She thrived within the church community that intertwined and enriched the relationships with her Caribbean neighbours.

My mother loved to help others, she was a very cheerful, uplifting and a loving soul. She gave big hugs; great advice and she had a huge heart; she was well loved in the community. Mother was also an excellent cook and her Caribbean cuisine became popular at the church summer fetes and at community events, promoted by organisations such as *Caribbean-Links*, a community-based initiative set up sometime during the late 1980s -1990s, headed by former Tottenham and late Labour party MP Bernie Grant. One of *Caribbean-Links* main objectives was *'to promote and defend the Caribbean and its cherished values, culture and family traditions'*.

Coming from a humble working-class background we didn't have a lot in terms of money or material things; but we made up for it with love, loyalty, extended family unity amongst our relatives and friends, added with gut wrenching laughter, good Caribbean food and music – reggae, ska, soca, jazz and R&B music. We also had the communal connectivity of our similar Caribbean backgrounds in common and to cling to. My brothers and I have fond memories of our childhood days and growing up in a close-knit Caribbean community. We always felt loved and protected from within this circle. And if you were larking about, as children often do, you better be on the look out from not just your parents but also your neighbours' parents too. As the African saying goes, it takes a village to raise a child.

The community was the village. Outside of the protective community bubble, living in London was often a harsher reality for many black Caribbeans.

I studied at North London University, graduating in 2002 with a BA Honours in Caribbean Studies and History. Following this, for seven years I worked for St. Mungo's, supporting and actively assisting homeless and vulnerable women to reestablish and reclaim their lives. In 2014, I completed a Master of Arts in Housing and Inclusion. In the final year of my Housing and Inclusion Master's Degree at London Metropolitan University, (formerly, North London University) I made the decision that the topic for my dissertation would be Caribbean Women's Migration and Windrush experiences inspired of my mother, and the rest as the saying goes is history.

BIBLIOGRAPHY

Alexander, Z., and Dewjee, A., 1999, *Wonderful Adventures of Mrs Seacole in Many Lands* (Bristol: Falling Wall Press).

Alleyne, B W., 2002, *Radicals against Race: Black Activism and Cultural Politics* (Oxford: Berg Publishers).

Barn, R., and Joseph Rowntree Foundation (JRF), 2001, *Black Youth on the Margins* (York: York Publishing Services Limited).

Benyon, J., 1986, *A Tale of Failure: Race and Policing* (Coventry: Centre for Research in Ethnic Relations).

Bourne, S., 2018, *War to Windrush: Black Women in Britain 1939 to 1948* (London: Jacaranda Books Art Music Ltd)

Bridge, G., and Watson, S., 2010, *The Blackwell City Reader, second edition* (Oxford: Wiley-Blackwell).

Bryan, B.; Dadzie, S.; and Scafe, S., 1985, *The Heart of the Race Black Women's Lives in Britain* (London: Virago Press Limited).

Burnett, P., ed., 1986, *The Penguin Book of Caribbean Verse in English* (London: Penguin Books Limited).

Bushnell, N., and Warren, C., 2010, *Edexcel GCSE History Controlled Assessment: CA11 Change in British Society 1955–75.* http://www.pearsonschoolsandfecolleges. co.uk/FEAndVocational/Humanities/History/EdexcelGCSEHistoryBSHP/Samples/ SampleControlledAssessmentMaterial/CA11ChangeinBritishsociety-Samplepages.pdf (accessed 20-07-13).

Carter, T., 1987, *Shattering Illusions: West Indians in British Politics* (London: Lawrence & Wishart Limited).

Cavendish, R., 1998, *Arrival of SS Empire Windrush*, History Today, 48:6. http:// www.historytoday.com/richard-cavendish/arrival-ss-empire-windrush (accessed 29-07-2014).

Christian, M., ed., 2002, *Black Identity in the 20th Century: Expressions of the US and UK African Diaspora* (London: Hansib Publications Limited).

Cobham, R., and Collins, M., eds., 1987, *Watchers & Seekers: Creative Writing by Black Women in Britain* (London: The Women's Press Limited).

Courtman, S., 2012, *Entertext: Women Writers and the Windrush Generation: A Contextual Reading of Beryl Gilroy's In Praise of Love and Children and Andrea Levy's Small Island.* www.brunel.ac.uk/data/assets/pdf_file/0006/198060/7_Courtman_Women-Writers-and-Windrush-Generation_FINAL.pdf (last accessed 27-07-2014).

Creswell, J. W., 2014, *Research Design: Qualitative, Quantitative, and Mixed Methods Approaches, fourth edition* (London: Sage Publications).

Davis, A. Y., 1982, *Women, Race & Class* (London: The Women's Press Ltd).

Department of Education and Science (DES), 1965, *Circular 7/65 (1965) The education of Immigrants,* http://www.educationengland.org.uk (accessed 23-08-2022)

Donnell, A., and Lawson Welsh, S., eds., 1996, *The Routledge Reader in Caribbean Literature* (London: Routledge).

Dookhan, I., 1975, *A Post Emancipation History of the West Indies* (London: Collins).

Elfman, elfman.co.uk (accessed 15-02-14).

Ellis, P., ed., 1986, *Women of the Caribbean* (London: Zed Books).

Fryer, P., 1984, *Staying Power: The History of Black People in Britain* (London: Pluto Press).

Gilroy, B., 1994, *Black Teacher,* (London: Bogle-L' ouverture Press Limited)

Going and Coming: Preserving Migration Stories, http://www.history.org.uk/resources/primary_resource_3461_65.html (accessed picture of Windrush Square 21-02-14).

Hackney.gov.uk, *Living Under One Roof—Windrush and Beyond* (Teacher's Pack), www.hackney.gov.uk/Assets/Documents/windrush-teachers-pack.pdf (accessed 3-07-2013).

Hall, S., Massey, D., Rustin, M., eds, 1998, *Soundings Issue 10 – Windrush Echoes* (London: Lawrence & Wishart)

Hamnett, C., and Butler, T., 2010, *The Changing Ethnic Structure of Housing Tenures in London, 1991–2001*, Urban Studies 47:1, 55–74, January.

Harrison, M., 1998, *Theorising Exclusion and Difference: Specificity, Structure and Minority Ethnic Issues*, Housing Studies 13:6, 793–806.

Harrison, M., with Phillips, D., 2003, *Housing and Black and Minority Ethnic Communities: Review of the Evidence Base* (London: Office of the Deputy Prime Minister).

Imperial War Museum, *Through My Eyes Stories of Conflict, Belonging and Identity,* http://www.throughmyeyes.org.uk/server/show/nav.22208 (accessed 27-03-14).

Institute of Race Relations, 1987, *Policing Against Black People* (Nottingham: Russell Press).

James, W., and Harris, C., eds, 1993, *Inside Babylon: The Caribbean Diaspora in Britain* (London: Verso Publishers).

Johnson, W.; Whyman, J.; and Wykes, G., 1968, *A Short Economic and Social History of Twentieth Century Britain.* (London: George Allen and Unwin Ltd).

Karatani, R., 2003, *Defining British Citizenship: Empire, Commonwealth, and Modern Britain* (London: Frank Cass).

Lewis, G., and Young, L., eds, 1998, *Windrush Echoes: Soundings Issue 10 Part II* (London: Lawrence & Wishart).

Lewis, R., and Bryan, P., eds, 1991, *Garvey His Work and Impact* (Trenton, New Jersey: Africa World Press, Inc.).

London Community Video Archive, 2018, *People's Account (1985),* www.the-lcva.co.uk/videos/5978 (last accessed 27-04-2022).

Lowe, S., 2011, *The Housing Debate* (Bristol: The Policy Press).

Lund, B., 2011, *Understanding Housing Policy Second Edition* (Bristol: The Policy Press).

Lund, B., 2016, *Housing Politics in the United Kingdom: Power, Planning and Protest* (Bristol: Policy Press)

MacEwen, M., 1991, *Housing, Race and Law: The British Experience* (London: Routledge).

McLeod, J., 2004, *Post Colonial London: Rewriting the Metropolis* (Oxfordshire: Routledge).

MoDA, Museum of Domestic Design & Architechure (Middlesex University), http://www.20thcenturylondon.org.uk/moda-badda2021 (accessed 16-02-14).

Mullard, C., 1973, *Black Britain* (London: George Allen & Unwin Limited).

Murdoch, A. H., 2012, *Creolizing the Metropole: Migrant Caribbean Identities in Literature and Film* (Bloomington, Indiana: Indiana University Press).

Nomis Official Labour Market Statistics and Office for National Statistics (ONS), Detailed Statistics, www.nomisweb.co.uk (accessed 26-03-14).

Office for National Statistics (ONS), *A Century of Home Ownership and Renting in England and Wales*, http://www.ons.gov.uk/ons/rel/census/2011-census-analysis/a-century-of-home-ownership-and-renting-in-england-and-wales/short-story-on-housing.html (accessed 27-07-2013).

Owusu, K., ed., 2000, *Black British Culture & Society A Text Reader* (London: Routledge).

Patterson, S., 1965, *Dark Strangers: a study of West Indians in London* (Middlesex, England: Pelican Books).

Peach, C., 1998, *South Asian and Caribbean Ethnic Minority Housing Choice in Britain*, Urban Studies 35:10, 1657–1680.

Peepaltreepress.com the best in Caribbean writing—Beryl Agatha Gilroy, http://www.peepaltreepress.com/author_display.asp?au_id=24 (last accessed 27-07-2014).

Phillips, D., 1998, *Black Minority Ethnic Concentration, Segregation and Dispersal in Britain*, Urban Studies, 35:10, 1681–1702, October.

Phillips, D., and Harrison, M., 2010, *Constructing an Integrated Society: Historical Lessons for Tackling Black and Minority Ethnic Housing Segregation in Britain,* Housing Studies 25:2, 221–235, February.

Phillips, M., 2011, *Windrush—the Passengers*, http://www.bbc.co.uk/history/british/modern/windrush_01.shtml (accessed 22-03-13).

Phillips, M., and Phillips, T., 1999, *Windrush, The Irresistible Rise of Multi-Racial Britain* (London: HarperCollins).

Port Cities, London, Historical events—Royal Museums Greenwich, http://www.portcities.org.uk/london/server/show/conMediaFile.1114/Ration-book-and-clothing-book.html, (accessed 16-02-14).

Read, A., ed., 1996, *The Fact of Blackness Fantz Fanon and Visual Representation* (London: ICA Publications).

Rex, J., and Moore, R., 1967, *Race Community and Conflict: A Study of Sparkbrook* (London: Oxford University Press).

Rodney, W., 2018, *How Europe Underdeveloped Africa* (London: Verso Publications)

Rutherford, A., 2020, *How to Argue with a Racist: History, Science, Race and Reality* (London: Weidenfeld & Nicolson)

Selvon, S., 1956, *The Lonely Londoners* (Harlow, Essex: Addison Wesley Longman Limited).

Selvon, S., 1990, *The Housing Lark*, (Washington, DC: Three Continents Press)

Sivanandan, A., 1982, *A Different Hunger: Writings on Black Resistance* (London: Pluto Press).

Solomos, J., 1993, *Race and Racism in Britain 2nd edition* (London: Macmillan Press Limited).

Somerville, P., and Steele, A., 2002, *"Race" Housing & Social Exclusion* (London: Jessica Kingsley Publishers Limited).

Spratt, V., 2022, *Tenants: The People on the Frontline of Britain's Housing Emergency* (London: Profile Books Ltd.)

Storey, J., ed., 1998, *Cultural Theory and Popular Culture A Reader: Second Edition* (Hertfordshire: Prentice Hall).

Swetnam, D., and Swetnam, R., 2000, *Writing Your Dissertation the Bestselling Guide to Planning, Preparing and Presenting First-Class Work. Third edition* (Oxford: How to Books Limited).

The Black Presence in Britain, http://www.blackpresence.co.uk – (accessed 26-07-2022)

Van Sertima, I., 1996, *African Presence in Early Europe.* (London: Transaction Publishers).

Voice-online, 2011, Pardna: Still Helping Hundreds Reach Their Savings Goals, www.voice-online.co.uk/article/pardna-still-helping-hundreds-reach-their-savings-goals (accessed 24-07-2014).

Wacquant, L., 2008, *Urban Outcasts: A Comparative Sociology of Advanced Marginality* (Cambridge: Polity Press).

West, J., ed., 1982, *Work, Women and the Labour Market* (London: Routledge & Kegan Paul Ltd).

Windrush Foundation Gallery, http://www.windrushfoundation.org/gallery-2/ (accessed 25-02-2014).

INDEX